COUNTED WORTHY

A Father's Perspective on the
Theology of Suffering

By
Connor R. Bales

VIDE

Vide Press
6200 Second Street
Washington D.C. 20011
www.VidePress.com

Print ISBN: 978-1-954618-24-4
eBook ISBN: 978-1-954618-25-1

Printed in the United States of America

Cover by Miblart.com

Dedication

This book is dedicated to God, who has counted our family worthy of the high calling to suffer for our own good and His great glory. Beyond that, I want to especially thank my incredible bride, Mary. She is the godliest woman I have ever known, and she has shown me what it means to love without condition – in her devotion to me, her care of our children, and her tenderness toward others around us.

I also want to express a special thanks to all five of my children. God has blessed me as a father and shown me a deeper understanding of love because of the wonderful uniqueness of each one of my kids. Finally, I want to thank my family and our friends. I have seen God's love most unexpectedly through the ministry of presence, patience, and prayer that my family and our friends have unreservedly shown to us. May God use this book to encourage others and remind us all that we have each been "Counted Worthy" of something. I pray Jesus is the hero of everything that happens because of this.

Table of Contents

Before You Begin...

When you are hurting, when you are down-for-the-count and nearly decimated, you might not be immediately drawn to a book that espouses a "theology of suffering." Your bruised heart doesn't want a systematic appraisal of affliction. Then again, this is no ordinary book on the subject. The essence of *Counted Worthy* springs from the tender heart of a wounded father.

Like its author Connor Bales, you may be a father. A dad who is sinking under the weight of a terrible disappointment that is crushing you and the ones you love. What is most bewildering is God. Right now, he doesn't seem to be the least bit trustworthy. And if you dare be honest, your faith in him is at risk of being shipwrecked.

However, something about this volume has captured your interest. It is a bold title, this: *Counted Worthy — A Father's Perspective on the Theology of Suffering*. But Connor Bales does not throw theology at you like a sucker punch. He does not serve up worn-out platitudes. He handles the topic of suffering carefully, cautiously, and with great sensitivity. It is because he, too, went through — no, he is *still* dealing with — unspeakable loss.

Connor and his wife Mary are parents to five amazing kids – two have significant disabilities. It's how I got to know the family. For years, the Bales clan has attended our Joni and Friends Family Retreats – five days of spiritual refreshment and hands-down, slam-dunk fun for special-needs families. Connor is also a pastor at Prestonwood Baptist Church in Dallas, and so he has served as our camp teacher. Connect those dots – he's a pastor and a special-needs dad. He *understands* the Bible, but he *really* understands the pain of disability.

The heart-wrenching condition of his two girls is all-consuming, and daily routines don't get easier. The medical outlook is not getting better. Every morning this dad wakes up to new and often harder challenges. When his first disabled child was born, Connor wrote, "God, why my child? She is innocent. Do you not see what she is going through? Why our family? We were doing the right things, being generous, and faithfully serving you."

The man who penned that does not expect you to gag down closely-reasoned arguments as to why God does things the way he does. That's not what this book is about. If anyone, Connor Bales understands that the hard sayings of Jesus can be *extremely* hard to swallow.

This is why *Counted Worthy* is such an unusual treatment on the subject of suffering. The author approaches it obliquely… on the tangent… not always head-on. He understands that an approach to suffering is shaped by the heart. Responses to gut-wrenching situations are always more determined by what is inside of a person than by the difficult things he is facing. While *Counted Worthy* may be filled with solid principles from the Bible, it is mostly filled with heart.

Yes, you'll be given a scriptural framework, but it is built out with helpful insights from wise people – things that helped Connor when he was at his lowest. He quotes Stephanie Hubach, a mom of a special-needs young adult... Matt Chandler, who survived brain cancer... Tim Keller and David Powlison, who both fought pancreatic cancer... and Elisabeth Elliot, the young missionary who went back to the jungle with a snakebite kit and her baby to serve among the very people that speared her husband to death. These sages know how to survive suffering, and Connor Bales gladly passes on their gems of wisdom.

I cannot say where you are on your path toward healing. You may feel heartsick beyond comforting, and if so, set aside this book until a better time. But if you are able, even though your pain is great, the Bible is full of encouragements to think, ponder, consider, weigh, and judge. It does this because how we view God influences our ability to move forward into life. The book you are holding in your hands tells me you want to move forward; *Counted Worthy* can help you do just that, and you could not have a better guide than its author.

So, somewhere in your busy household, carve out a little space, grab a yellow highlighter (you'll want one by the third chapter), and allow the wounded father with the tender heart to lead you. For this is no ordinary book on the subject of suffering.

Joni Eareckson Tada
Joni and Friends International Disability Center
Agoura Hills, California

Introduction

I'm a Texan. I was born in Texas, I have always lived in Texas, and while my wife, Mary, and I love to travel and see other parts of the country and our world, I must admit that I am always most comfortable in Texas. Now, I tell you that because one thing that seems to be somewhat unique to Texas is the variety and unpredictability of our weather. The sheer size of our state means we experience the widest variety of climate conditions. There are some parts of Texas that experience the bitter cold in winter, like the plain states of middle America, while at the same time, those living in our southernmost parts of the state will be wearing T-shirts and shorts. I have always heard the saying of Texas weather, *"If you don't like it, just wait fifteen minutes for it to change."*

I tell you this because a few years ago when my family and I lived in Longview, Texas, we experienced one of those crazy Texas weather days. In fact, on that day, we had a very unusual snowstorm. On this particular morning, much to my kids' delight, we woke up to a snow-covered winter wonderland. There were several inches of snow covering the ground, greeting everyone when we woke up, ready for school and work.

This unexpected weather, then led to the dilemma that day. You see, in Texas (most especially East Texas), snow is relatively rare and enough snow for any significant accumulation is even rarer still. And because snow is so rare for us, most Texans don't know how to drive in it. Admittedly, we just don't naturally navigate snow and icy road conditions well, primarily because, unlike our brothers and sisters from up North, we don't see it often enough.

When we woke up that day, we immediately noticed all of the local school and business closings in our area, so in an abundance of caution, we followed suit and closed our office as well, to keep staff off the roads and ensure that everyone could stay safe and warm. I, however, knew I needed to get some work done, so I quickly drove up to the office to grab my laptop so that I could work from home that day. I drive a four-wheel-drive pickup truck, so for me to navigate the road conditions wasn't really a problem.

Having said that, I wasn't on the road very long before I realized that not everyone else was navigating the snowy roads as successfully as I was. In fact, on my way out, I noticed that at the intersection directly behind my house, several cars had stalled or spun out, trying unsuccessfully to make their way to work. By the time I returned home from getting my laptop at the office, at least six cars at that intersection near home were sideways, wrecked, spun out, or veered off the road and stranded. I quickly parked my truck in the driveway, went inside to put on some warmer clothes and I then headed back out to help push, pull, and assist these stranded motorists in any way that I could.

I spent the rest of that morning helping the parade of drivers who didn't heed the warnings and instead attempted to make their way to work, only to find themselves stuck or stranded by the snow and ice covering the road. It wasn't what I had planned to do that morning, but I knew I needed to try and help out in any way I could. I just wanted to help. In fact, as much as I knew that I hadn't planned on helping stranded drivers that day, I also knew that none of those who found themselves in the ditch started their morning or their week or their year with that plan on their agenda for that day either. Nevertheless, it happened. An unexpected snowstorm showed up and the roads immediately became impassable, creating the ensuing disaster that so many unsuspecting motorists found themselves facing that day.

It has been my experience that sometimes life works in a similar way. Most of us have ideas, dreams, and plans for how we think, pray, and hope our life is going to work. But, if you've lived much of it, you already know that it rarely ends up as it started out. Unexpected snowstorms can show up and will spin us out and leave us crashed in the ditch. It just seems to be this way. In our broken world, things don't always work as God originally designed and therefore, most of us have spent some time of our lives trying to get out of the ditch and back on the road to wherever it is we are trying to go.

Mary and I have been in the ditch. Our first big storm hit on October 6, 2008 when we had our third child, our daughter Libby. And since Libby's birth, we've spun out more than a few times, which is why I am writing this book. Like that morning with those stranded motorists, I just want to help. My hope and prayer is that if you have found yourself in the ditch or you're trying to get back on the road after crashing into it, perhaps our story of God's grace toward us in the midst of our storms can serve as an encouragement to you. I know this … life will spin you out sometimes. Storms are a part of life.

Our family has experienced more than one storm, and judging by the unpredictability of life's weather, we will probably be hit with a few more before it's all done. Jesus spoke of this reality in Matthew 7:24–27 (ESV), when He said, *"Everyone then who hears these words of mine and does them will be like a wise man who built his house on the rock.* ***And the rain fell, and the floods came, and the winds blew*** *and beat on that house, but it did not fall, because it had been founded on the rock. And everyone who hears these words of mine and does not do them will be like a foolish man who built his house on the sand.* ***And the rain fell, and the floods came, and the winds blew*** *and beat against that house, and it fell, and great was the fall of it."*

Jesus said the rains fall, the floodwaters rise, and the wind blows hard. It's a fact. Bad weather is coming, and storms are in life's forecast. This is a part of life and sometimes that stormy weather will spin you out, cause you to crash, or leave you stranded as you try to navigate the journey of your life. Our family has been in the ditch more than once, and you can bet we will end up spun out a few more times still. But we're learning how to drive in the weather and perhaps by our transparency, you can be better served for your road trips in life as well. And the good news for you and me is that God's Word is not silent on the subject of suffering. Author Paul David Tripp explains it this way, "Scripture never looks down on the sufferer, it never mocks his pain, it never turns a deaf ear to his cries, and it never condemns him for his struggle. It presents to the sufferer a God who understands, who cares, who invites us to come to him for help, and who promises one day to end all suffering of any kind once and forever. Because of this, the Bible, while being dramatically honest about suffering, is at the same time gloriously hopeful. And it's not just that the Bible tells the story of suffering honestly and authentically; it also gives us concrete and real hope." [1]

In the same way, Pastor Matt Chandler speaks about the honesty found in God's Word when he writes, "The Bible isn't full of clean happy living. You could argue that it's a book more full of tears than smiles. It's full of God working for the good of his people in the mess brought about by sin and death. God is with his people through suffering and through difficulty, so that they come out on the other side as a picture of grace and glory, and he uses them in their pain and changes the world through the results of their trials. You're not really thinking, 'This person is going to be a big deal here' ... and they become a big deal in God's story. Take Bathsheba again—taken advantage of by a powerful man, her king; and then God weaves her into the ancestry of the Son of God, her Savior and ours, the Lord Jesus. The suffering is not belittled, and the crime is not excused, yet God weaves it into his great story of salvation of hope.

"We see the same thing throughout church history. Suffering is everywhere. Just to look back to the last 500 years and some of the more famous names, John Owen experienced the death of eleven children. Jonathan Edwards struggled with painful gout and then died at the young age of 55 after a smallpox inoculation had led to him contracting the disease shortly after he was named the president of Princeton University. Charles Spurgeon bore the weight of debilitating depression. John Calvin wrestled with digestion problems nearly his whole life. David Brainerd died of tuberculosis. And the list continues. To this day, most of the men and women I know whom God seems to be using in profound ways have endured or continue to endure 'trials of various kinds.' The twentieth-century theologian A.W. Tozer once said, 'It is doubtful whether God can bless a man greatly until he has hurt him deeply.' At forty-three, I have seen this to be true.

"But what I've found to be unique about the biblical perspective is not only that suffering is a reality but that joy in that suffering can be a reality too. Chapter 1 of the book of James not only assumes that we will face trials and tribulations as Christians but argues that these sufferings are a pathway to maturity, showing us that we lack nothing that we truly need. It's the idea that for us to bear fruit in our lives, we will probably need the plow. We need something to wake us up, to stir us up, to make us rely more on the Lord, and look more like Jesus. And so when we walk into a trial, we can know 'joy' there. There can be smiles in the tears.

"Everyone will suffer. You're either suffering now, or you will be suffering in the future. As Christians, regardless of how faithful and obedient we are, we'll have seasons in which the sky is clear, and we'll have seasons in which it's cloudy. And one day we'll face the end of our seasons here. Everybody knows they're going to die, but nobody thinks it's this year." [2]

Chandler concludes this thought by saying, "In dark and difficult seasons—when we face pain and suffering, when we get that one phone call that changes everything—we may not know or understand everything, but we can trust that the Lord is leading us into maturity and showing us that we need him. And we can also trust that, by his Spirit and through his church, he is not going to abandon us; he is with us. He is encouraging us and he is giving us what we need to walk through that suffering faithfully." [3]

In any case, it is never lost on me, and as we begin, I don't want it to be lost on you ... Jesus is always with us! He is right next to us in every spin out, stall out, and wreck out we will ever face. God is in the ditch, right beside you. Tripp explains it like this, "In an indescribable act of unmerited grace, he has made you the place where he lives, and in the faithfulness of that grace he will never walk away from you. In your suffering, you will again and again fail to say or do the right thing. Under the weight of difficulty, you will lose your way for a while. You will drag yourself out of bed only to have a debilitating day of spiritual struggle. You will get very sad or very mad. One moment you will long for people to be with you and the next moment wish they would leave you alone. You won't always be comforted by the words of your loved ones, and there will be moments when you will wish they'd stop saying the things they say. Sometimes you will rest in God's rule, and other times you will be haunted by the future.

"But in all the emotional and spiritual ups and downs, on the good days and the bad days, when you fight or succumb, one thing is for sure. Your Lord is with you, and there is no struggle without or war within that will ever drive him away. And his presence guarantees that in your suffering, you will have everything you need." [4]

I'll remind you of what Moses reminded Joshua in the Old Testament book of Deuteronomy, just before Joshua would lead God's people in Moses' absence: *"It is the LORD who goes before you. He will be with you; he will not leave you or forsake you. Do not fear or be dismayed."* (Deuteronomy 31:8 ESV).

Chapter 1
"CRASH"

It was a typical Saturday morning around the Bales' home.
Other than Mary being out of town for a very rare girls'
weekend getaway, things were not unusual in any way.
We had enjoyed a good week, our kids were doing well
in school and the Bales family was enjoying a wonderful
spring season in East Texas. I woke up on this particular
Saturday ready for a great weekend ahead, and I began to
go about my morning routine.

Our routine each morning is not like everyone else's, I would
imagine, but it is pretty simple and it is definitely what works
for us. Mary and I always start our days by checking in on
our middle daughters, Libby and Hannah. Most mornings
at least one of the girls is awake early and babbling in her
bed, waiting for someone to come in and say hello. This is
always a highlight of my day! I've always said that, if Libby
and Hannah smiling and babbling and talking can't put you
in a good mood, then nothing can because there is nothing
sweeter than those girls making those sounds (I might
admittedly be biased—not sure). Now, because our girls
have such severe special needs and accompanying health
complications, they have almost always had a bedroom very
near to ours—so we can check in on them and administer
feedings and medications as easily as possible for all.

However, this morning, things were anything but normal. With both girls having slept quietly through the night, I went in to check on them and noticed that Hannah was very pale and appeared to be very labored in her breathing. I understand that for most parents this would immediately be alarming, and I'll admit that I was not comfortable with how Hannah seemed, but because the girls have both had a history of pneumonia, Mary and I are well versed in administering rescue breathing treatments in an attempt to open their airway and slow their breathing down to an acceptable rate. In other words, this scene was not the first time we had witnessed one of the girls struggling with some type of respiratory distress. That said, given just how labored Hannah's breathing was that morning, I quickly assembled the medicine into the nebulizer machine and began to administer this treatment, hoping she would bounce back quickly and her respirations would slow down and become less labored.

Unfortunately, the treatment didn't work. I knew that I was going to need to take her to the hospital so she could be seen right away. I quickly called a babysitter to come over and stay with the other children so I could get Hannah to the emergency room. I then scooped Hannah into my arms and out of her bed so that I could lay her on our bed, in our room, and change her diaper and get her dressed and ready to leave. It was at this point when it set in for me just how sick she was and just how distressed her little body might actually be. As I picked her up to carry her, I noticed that Hannah was completely limp. She was not only having difficulty with her breathing, but she was almost entirely unresponsive to my moving her, and my talking to her seemed not to register with her in any way at all. This was now very scary and things were moving from bad to worse very quickly.

Our babysitter arrived promptly thereafter and agreed that Hannah looked very distressed. I loaded her into her car seat and began to rush off to the emergency room for help. Just before leaving, my oldest daughter Kathryn, who was fourteen years old at the time, was awake and downstairs, no doubt hearing the commotion as I was preparing to leave with Hannah. Seeing the distressed look on her face, I invited her to ride with me to take Hannah to the hospital. I knew that Kathryn was very concerned and I could use the help of someone sitting in the back with Hannah while I sped to the hospital as fast as I could.

In the flurry of calling the babysitter and while trying to see if the breathing treatment at home would help, I also called a close personal friend who was an emergency room doctor to ask his opinion for treatment and next steps and to determine which local hospital to go to for the fastest treatment that day. Based on my description of Hannah and having seen her in emergency respiratory failures in the past, he directed me to take her to the hospital right away and gave me instructions as to where to go for care on that particular day. He agreed to call ahead to the hospital as well, so that we might be seen right away and to help assist the attending physician with a little background information as someone who had cared for Hannah in similar situations in her past.

So Kathryn, Hannah, and I took off. While we raced to the hospital I called Mary to tell her that Hannah was very sick and that we were heading in to be seen. Mary is an incredible mother and knows the drill with our girls better than any of us. She sprang into action from out of town and rallied her friends to be ready to leave in the event this was going to be a longer stay or a crisis of any type. Kathryn did her best to talk to Hannah in the back seat while we drove, holding her head up in the car seat as her little body was too limp to do anything on its own. Panic was beginning to settle in for us.

We were immediately rushed back into a room. Undoubtedly because of the call ahead from our doctor friend and also given the very visibly distressed condition of Hannah herself, we immediately drew the attention of a physician and several emergency room nurses as well. They hooked Hannah up for monitoring and to take her vitals to determine what her condition looked like right then. I knew it was bad right away because while the average person has an oxygen saturation rate of about 96% breathing room air, Hannah's was registering at 67%. The doctor also noticed that Hannah's heart was racing too fast and that she had spiked a high fever. Her condition was so alarming that we were quickly moved into one of the trauma bays.

Not long after being moved into the trauma room, Hannah began having multiple seizures and the doctor informed me that he was going to need to intubate Hannah to assist her with her breathing. This was shocking because, despite all of the pneumonia she had suffered in the past, it was something we had never experienced before. The doctor also told me that after he stabilized her, he would immediately begin making plans to have Hannah flown by helicopter to a children's hospital in Dallas where she could receive more specialized care.

I knew this was the most serious illness we had yet faced with our girls—Hannah had crashed. I stepped out into the hallway and called Mary to update her on things and to tell her that she should do whatever she could to meet us in Dallas right away. I couldn't explain things very eloquently, but when I said that "Hannah had crashed," Mary knew exactly how dire the situation truly was.

To make matters worse, my poor Kathryn was standing in the trauma room watching the medical team work furiously on Hannah the entire time. They started IVs in both her arms and began administering fluids and antibiotics, along with medicine aimed at stopping the seizures. I have mixed feelings about exposing Kathryn to that trauma that day. The truth is, I needed her help in transporting Hannah to the hospital and I certainly didn't know how bad things were going to get, but I am confident that witnessing the stress of that day, the tragedy of watching her little sister suffer and the significance of those events, has forever marked our eldest—I pray that by God's grace, He uses it for good.

Both Kathryn and I were crying as the doctor made his first attempt at intubating Hannah. If you've never witnessed this being done, it is a very difficult process to watch, especially when it's being attempted on your helpless, lifeless, six-year-old little girl. I remember standing at the end of the bed while a nurse was breathing for Hannah with a compression bag. The team would watch the monitors carefully and when they felt her oxygen saturation was high enough for another attempt, the doctor would use a device to insert a tube deep into her throat, allowing oxygen to reach her lungs. The attending physician was having a very difficult time getting Hannah intubated. I'm not sure if the pressure of her dad standing at the end of the bed weeping or the difficulty of navigating Hannah's airway or the fragility of that moment, in particular, created such a problem, but despite his best effort, he was not successful try after try.

As I began to grow discouraged, heading toward despair, my friend (the doctor I spoke to earlier in the day) walked into the room. He was dressed in street clothes as he had been off that day and was actually attending his kid's soccer games that morning when I called. He calmly walked into the intensity of that room, carefully, but quickly, washed his hands and put on sterile gloves, walked over to his associate and offered help. With collegial kindness and respect, my friend immediately assisted and was able to successfully intubate Hannah. They hooked her up to a respirator and within a few minutes Hannah's breathing began to slow and her heart rate began to calm.

I'll never forget the sheer intensity of that moment. My friend walked over to me, seeing my hysteria and despair, he gently placed his hand on my shoulder and said, "Connor, at least we can get her to Dallas now." Clearly, he was unable to communicate that Hannah would be okay, but he was able to assure me that she wouldn't die right now.

At this point, I had called my closest friend who I served with on staff at our church in East Texas. He was out of town himself, but he quickly worked the phones on my behalf and a few close friends from our church and staff had begun to gather in the hospital room with us. They were doing their best to console Kathryn and me, while the doctors and the medical team continued to try to stabilize Hannah and make provision for her transport to Dallas as soon as arrangements could be made.

Hannah's seizures were still active and so more medicine was administered in an attempt to slow them down, the result however was that Hannah was almost completely sedated and from a physically observable perspective, with all of the tubes and machines connected to her frail little body, she looked terrible. This was a low point in my life. This was a low point for our family. I was convinced we were going to lose my daughter that day.

To make matters worse, the crazy Texas weather had decided to prove itself unpredictable yet again. Spring thunderstorms were rolling across North and East Texas that day and securing an air ambulance for Hannah's travel to Dallas was proving very difficult for the medical team. First, a helicopter was ruled out because the weather would not allow it. Next, a single wing airplane was eliminated because it would have had to fly too far around to avoid the weather as well. Finally, the children's hospital in Dallas elected to send their specialty care flight crew via ground ambulance to Longview, our East Texas hometown, to pick her up and bring her back to Dallas directly, under their care and specialized supervision.

What began that morning had turned into a very long day. It was now Saturday evening and we were finally heading to Dallas. Friends had taken Kathryn home and care was being arranged for our other four children at home. I was following the care flight ambulance on the highway headed for Dallas. Mary, and the group of ladies she had been out of town with, drove straight from their getaway to Dallas and met us at the hospital there. Hannah's crash had sent our entire family, church, and friend network into overdrive. If a community can feel collective pain, ours certainly did that day.

They rushed Hannah through the emergency room at the children's hospital in Dallas and we were immediately sent upstairs to the pediatric intensive care unit (PICU) where we met a wonderful pediatric intensivist who began to immediately give attention to Hannah and assess her condition. Hannah's intubation tube had somehow gotten clogged as we arrived at the hospital and as a result, her breathing began to grow dangerously fast again just as she was being taken to her room. The doctor immediately stepped in and reintubated her with a new tube and hooked her up to the respirator and turned the oxygen support to a very high level. Hannah began to calm back down and her breathing regulated once again. Mary was in the room this time, distraught with worry and fear, just like me. She got a glimpse in that moment of what our entire day had been and the up-and-down nature of this medical crisis our little girl was fighting with her life.

Once stabilized, the doctor visited with Mary and me and told us what she thought the next twenty-four hours might look like for our little girl. She simply described Hannah as being "very sick" and told us that, with her underlying conditions, things were far too fragile to predict right now. She was very kind and tender toward us, seeing our distress and concern. She allowed us to kiss Hannah goodnight and then recommended we go upstairs for some rest where the hospital had made arrangements for us to have a courtesy room.

Things progressed very slowly for Hannah in the weeks to follow. Her condition worsened after the first week and the pneumonia wrecked her little body with infection. At one point, under the direction of our doctors, I made a trip home to Longview and pulled my oldest two children out of school to talk with them and let them know that it didn't look like their sister was going to pull through. That's the hardest conversation I have ever had to have and one no parent ever should.

Hannah's seizures were difficult to control as her infection lowered her body's threshold to fight them. On one particularly difficult day, she was recorded as having more than forty seizures every hour. Hannah had a stroke while she was in the hospital when she was the sickest. It affected the left side of her body, especially her fine motor skills—which weren't great even before. This illness had crushed my daughter. This illness had crushed our family. Friends from both Dallas and back home in East Texas were regular visitors for the month we stayed in the hospital. Because Mary and I alternated every few days between the hospital and home, our family had dinners a few times in the lobby of the children's hospital so that my oldest kids could see their sister and we could all be together, even if just only for a few hours at a time.

But God was merciful. After a few weeks, the doctors believed Hannah was stable enough to begin weaning down on the required oxygen and after a couple of failed attempts, Hannah was able to be removed from the intubation and respirator. Although it sounds simple, this is a process to be sure. First, Hannah transitioned to a BiPAP respirator and then finally to a nasal cannula oxygen requirement alone. Physical therapists began working to restore some of Hannah's lost muscle tone and to combat the atrophy which had riddled her body. After thirty-two days in the PICU, Hannah came home.

Our little girl wasn't the same for a long time. It has been more than three years since that crash on that Saturday, and we still haven't gotten back all that was lost. But Hannah is alive. God spared our daughter that day—and my gratitude and joy couldn't be properly expressed for the mercy that we have received through the kindness and nearness of God. Storms are a part of life. I know that and so do you. Our family has endured a lot of them through the years and I am certain we will fight through a few more as well. When Hannah crashed in the spring of 2018, it was a category-five storm for us. We have fought, cried, thrown our hands up, and felt entirely lost on more occasions than I can recall. But we've never sat in the storms alone. Everyone will crash at some point. On that day, Hannah crashed and so did I. But this is not how our story began...

Chapter 2

"CHARMED"

Looking back now, that is how I would have described the life Mary and I had as newlyweds and as a young family, it was "charmed." Now, I certainly don't mean that we were (or are) perfect. I think the balance of this book will make that more than clear, but our life was a good one. By most of the western, especially American, standards in the South, we were doing great and living a "charmed life." Allow me to explain…

Mary and I met in high school while working at a summer camp in Leakey, Texas, in the summer of 1994. The camp was Laity Lodge Youth Camp (LLYC), and it was an incredible place for young people to have an awesome spiritual encounter with God in the most fun environment imaginable. Mary served on the work crew, primarily preparing the lunchroom for meals, serving the campers during the meals, and cleaning the lunchroom after meals. I worked on the kitchen crew. Yes, as scary as this sounds to anyone who knows me, I helped prepare and cook the meals. In fact, there are probably still some very scarred individuals from a botched attempt at brownies that I became somewhat infamous for that summer.

This was the summer before our senior year of high school and when we met at camp, we quickly became fast friends. While we both were dating other people back in our respective hometowns, we had a connection to one another that was strong and proved to be binding. I instantly had a crush on Mary, and although it's a little embarrassing to admit, Mary insists that she simply thought I was funny and a nice guy to make friends with while at camp. I remember vividly sitting out on the tennis courts at night, after our work responsibilities had ended, and simply hanging out as a group with kitchen and work staff. The sky was beautiful, the weather was great, and the conversations were full of laughter, but honestly, I was never interested in it unless I knew Mary was going to be there. I was crazy about her from the beginning.

After camp ended, we stayed in contact during our senior year of high school by writing letters to one another. (For those of you born after 1990, handwritten letters, mailed via the United States Postal Service, were our least expensive means of communication. Long-distance calling was costly, and our parents limited them greatly. On top of that, email was relatively unknown and text messaging was not yet around. So, letters were our thing.) Mary lived in Katy, Texas, a suburb just outside of Houston and I lived in Coppell, Texas, a suburb just outside of Dallas. In addition to our letters, we were able to see each other over the Christmas break in the fall of 1994, which was great!

In the busyness of that spring of our senior year, our letters became less frequent and our phone calls even more so. By the time we were heading off to college for our freshman year, we had lost touch with one another.

I spent my freshman year at Southwestern University in Georgetown, Texas, where I played basketball and Mary attended Texas Tech University in Lubbock. We didn't connect at all our freshman year and it seemed that our friendship had run its course.

I decided, after the frustration of an injury and some serious freshman immaturity, that I would transfer as a sophomore to Texas Tech and study landscape architecture. This transition made sense to me as Texas Tech was where my dad had attended in the 1960s and from where my older brother Jayson had recently graduated only a year before. I had a family connection with the university and had always grown up a Red Raider fan. My decision to transfer made even more sense as I had a number of friends at Tech already and so I thought the transition would be a good one academically and relatively smooth socially.

In late August or early September of 1996, during my first weekend in Lubbock, I ran back into Mary at a party. I couldn't believe it. What an awesome surprise! While I knew Mary was a student at Tech, I didn't think we would see one another or likely run in the same circles. Likewise, Mary was so shocked to see me that she actually confused me with my older brother Jayson, who she had seen some the year before when she was a freshman and he was a senior. For us, the connection was instant and beyond exciting, and while Mary was dating someone at that time, I wasted no time in letting her know of my feelings about her and I worked quickly to move that other guy out of the picture. We began dating in the fall of our sophomore year and fell in love right away.

With the exception of a few months, Mary and I dated throughout our time in college and were engaged on the weekend of her graduation in May of 1999. We had, in my opinion, a Hollywood-ready love story. We met in high school and had an instant connection. We then tragically lost touch after our senior year (cue the sad music). We reconnected in dramatic fashion almost two years after losing touch, fell madly in love, and were engaged (cue the celebration and love music). Okay, maybe it's not Hollywood ready, but it's our story just the same and I can say today, having been married twenty-one years as I am writing this book, I am without a doubt more in love with that girl from summer camp than I've ever been before. It is no exaggeration for me to say that apart from my salvation by faith in Jesus Christ, Mary is the greatest gift God has ever given to me and I am overwhelmed by the continued blessing she is to me and to our entire family. Now, let me get back to our "charmed" story...

At Texas Tech, the landscape architecture program was for almost all students a five-year program, and as a transfer, it most certainly was for me. So in the spring of 1999, when Mary was getting out, I still had another year of school before I would graduate. Mary was a social work major in school and upon graduation began working at the University Medical Center as a hospital social worker on their staff. She was primarily working in the ER, burn unit, and post-surgical floor. That last year of school went by so slowly for me as Mary was already out and enjoying life after studying and we were planning our wedding for July of 2000, which would come very quickly after my graduation in May of the same year. Our parents were incredibly supportive as we planned the wedding and worked toward life after college. Our "charmed" life was beginning to take shape.

Mary and I were married on July 1, 2000 at St. Justin Martyr Catholic Church in Houston. We honeymooned at Lake Tahoe and upon our return had rented an apartment in a brand-new complex in Grapevine, Texas, the neighboring suburb to Coppell. I had gotten a good job with a small landscape design/build company in Coppell and likewise, Mary had found a good job working as a social worker assisting a local school district on the outskirts of the DFW metroplex.

We quickly settled ourselves into the comfortable and affluent suburban American life. We found a great local church, made great friendships, and were climbing the ladders of success in our respective careers. Life was good. We were earning well, living well, and things seemed to be heading in a smooth and successful direction. As newlyweds and DINKs (Double Income with No Kids) we took fun vacations, had great date nights, and sometimes, Saturdays mostly, we had date days! We were living a "charmed" life, and it only got better...

We were blessed with our first child, our daughter Kathryn on March 8, 2004. She was an unbelievable blessing and while Mary and I had both always known we wanted children, it wasn't until Kathryn's arrival that I knew how much joy and fun being a dad and parent could actually be. That girl did, and still does, have me wrapped around her finger. Things were great. Kathryn was great. She was an easy baby and because things were going so well in my business, Mary was able to give herself primarily to staying at home and being available for Kathryn.

During these years of starting our family, Mary and I also started a business. Having earned my degree in landscape architecture and then gaining a good deal of experience by working for several small to medium-sized landscape design, build, and maintenance companies in and around Dallas, we boldly struck out on our own and formed 3B Landscape Development, Inc. We started our very own landscape design, build, and maintenance company, from scratch. This was an exciting time for our family, but if I'm being honest, somewhat scary as well. With a new baby at home and the pressure of being the primary financial provider for the family, we desperately needed our venture to succeed.

It did!

Our family was very blessed and fortunate that our company launched with great success and within two years I was given an opportunity to merge 3B with a much larger landscape company in Dallas, where I would earn an equity position as a part-owner and where I would be given the daily responsibilities of General Manager for the entire business. Obviously, this served as an incredible springboard for my career. Becoming a part-owner of this much larger firm provided us a long-term financial posture that would have otherwise taken many years to earn. Now, like any other business person, every day wasn't great. There were ups and downs, tensions with teammates, and trouble with clients, but overall, the business was booming and things were generally moving in the right direction. We were blessed indeed. You might say our life was, "Charmed."

We were still figuring the parenting thing out and navigating the daily battles of running a business, but we were managing well and, from our perspective, our life was by the measurable "American Christian" standards, a very successful one. I use the term "American Christian" very cautiously. I don't mean it to be offensive to anyone, after all, I am a Christian who lives in America. I'm both grateful for my salvation from God that makes me a Christian and I count myself as very fortunate to be born in America, an incredible country where our freedom is not cheap, but priceless. But, when I say that our life was successful by measurable "American Christian" standards, I mean that for a western Christian who is, by whole-world standards, exceedingly blessed financially and medically, in respect to available healthcare and based upon general living conditions, I mean that we were prospering even according to those American norms.

Mary and I had always said, even from our years of dating and engagement in college, that we wanted to have five children. Clearly today, I can say as the father of five children, that we had no idea what we were asking or what was in store. I think our general conviction was that we knew we wanted a larger family, with several children. Of course, knowing what I do today, I am even more convinced that it is God's sovereignty alone that determines how many children a family may or may not be given and by what means. Some families have children naturally and other families are given children supernaturally, through foster care and adoption, and

I completely believe it is by God's grace that all families are formed.

But Mary and I tried and were blessed to continue growing our family and our son, Coleman, was born on September 21, 2006, and again, we were beyond excited! Coleman was, and still is, Mister Easy Going. I was so excited to have a son. Mary and I have both known from the earliest days that he and I would share a closeness that, still to this day, is incredibly binding as father and son.

"Charmed." That's how I would have described our life. Easy pregnancies, easy babies, our life was good. We had a very nice, big home with a swimming pool in the backyard. I was earning more money than I ever imagined. We were giving generously to and faithfully attending our local church. We had great friendships and our young family was incredibly healthy and happy. "Charmed." Things just seemed to be going our way.

Again, let me be clear on this, our life was not perfect. Mary and I are NOT perfect. We had our share of arguments as husband and wife, frustrations as Mom and Dad, tensions with family and friends, and letdowns as a business leader and owner, but overall, things just seemed good. Really, really good.

Given how good things were going, and knowing we both wanted a large family, we decided we would try for a another child. The growth of our family wasn't always easy, and we have had two sad and disappointing miscarriages at various times. Mary became pregnant yet again with what would be our third child, a girl. I couldn't wait to see how our "charmed" life would take shape next.

Chapter 3
"CALLED"

I have to admit, ten years into my vocational life in
ministry, there are still days when I cannot believe that this
is the life God has chosen for me. Don't get me wrong,
that is not a statement of disappointment or dissatisfaction.
I love serving the local church as a minister of the Gospel
of Jesus Christ and I consider myself blessed to serve.
I absolutely love being a pastor and cannot imagine doing
anything else. I love the church where I serve, the staff
with whom I serve, and the role that has been entrusted to
me to fulfill. I simply mean that there are times when what
I do, as a vocational minister, seems to be the furthest thing
from what I thought I'd be doing. This ministry life that
we live is not how I diagrammed our "charmed" life to be.

Allow me a few minutes to share with you my journey of
faith. I think my story will help give context to the life
that Mary and I now live, the faith and strength by which
we live it, the vulnerable transparency that is required for
it, and the hope that we have despite all of the challenges
that come with it. Additionally, I sincerely pray that as you
read about my relationship with God through Jesus, you
might be able to take some time to contemplate your own
relationship with God. Perhaps by reflecting on my story,
you could ask God to make clear your own. Ask yourself,

"What do I believe?", "In whom do I believe?", "Where do I find my hope?", "Do I even believe in God?", "Can I honestly say I have and enjoy a relationship with Him?"

The Bible is clear that God is personal, and desires to encounter each and every one of us in a personal way. So perhaps you're reading this book because someone recommended it to you as a means of encouragement in your season of suffering. Maybe you're in life's storm and you've found yourself spun out in a ditch. Maybe you have heard of our story or about our family and wanted to discover the details for yourself. Perhaps you're simply using this book as a time waste on a vacation, plane flight, or to escape the awkward dialogue with the in-laws at a family gathering. Whatever has led to your reading this, I hope and pray that our story, from my faith to our future, will generate some thought-provoking introspection into your story. I hope you will take the time to make sure of what you believe and in whom you trust. I am praying that this book might solidify what is certain, or that it might lead you to ask questions and discover God's answers for what is available to you from a God who undoubtedly loves you.

You see, my journey of faith begins early in my life. My first memories of church or the things of God are vivid for me. I was fortunate enough to be born into a family with a mom and dad who both loved and worshipped Jesus faithfully for all of my life. While neither was perfect, as either would have said themselves, my parents were committed Christ-followers who attended the local church, served in the local church, and supported the local church for all of their married lives.

My father became a Christian, placing his faith in Jesus, as a junior in high school. While his road with God was up and down, my dad's salvation was sure and he was good to shepherd my two brothers and me into the importance of faith and the forgiveness of sin that comes through Jesus Christ alone.

My mother became a Christian when she was pregnant with me. Having been raised as a very proper, conservative, religious woman, it wasn't until she was confronted with the truth of repentance and God's available forgiveness that she was transformed by the grace of God through Jesus. My mom jokingly takes great credit for my calling into vocational ministry as being linked back to her conversion to Christ while pregnant with me.

So, having grown up in a family of faith, my relationship with and knowledge of God existed from a very early age. That said, however, I didn't understand the personal reality that a saving relationship with God should entail, until much later in my life. I knew about God to be sure, but I didn't have a personal relationship with Him.

My parents had my brothers and me in church for all of our lives. We were socially and morally conservative Christians, through and through. In fact, I have some memories I'm still working through that include "alternative Halloween celebrations" for those families (like ours) who were looking to avoid mainstream devils and demons, as my mom feared we might be corrupted by them. While my buddies were dressing up as their favorite athletes and superheroes, there were several Halloweens when I had cotton balls glued to my face with Elmer's school glue, while I dressed up as Moses or another hero from the Old Testament of the Bible (Yes, this is absolutely frightening and true.). This incredible parental feat of taking the fun out of Halloween was accomplished by cutting a hole in a large brown bath towel, tying a thin rope around the waist, wearing a beige or plain white undershirt, wearing khaki shorts (for modesty, of course), and completing the ensemble with brown sandals. All of this, in great cooperation with the aforementioned cotton-ball beard, would ensure that the outfit looked the part. But, I'm over it ... sort of.

Now, before you choose to stop reading, or try finding my email address so you can share with me all of the values of a good fall festival and the dangers of Halloween, please don't do that either. I get it. I'm aware as a Christian, dad, and pastor of the dangers of evil and the real spiritual battles with the demonic. I'm also aware of the Reformation and the invaluable work of Martin Luther. I'm simply sharing what I think is a funny memory of growing up in my family of faith. So, I'm not opposed to Fall Festivals or Halloween parties, so long as the Gospel of Christ isn't compromised in either celebration or that fun isn't programmed out of the event. Now, back to my childhood...

Despite the scarring "Moses memory", my parents were incredible people who loved Jesus very much and did a wonderful job of sharing with us God's goodness, His provision, His forgiveness, and our need for His grace. That said, I still grew up with a warped understanding that my relationship with God was as dependent upon my behavior and external actions as it was God's goodness given to me. This mindset led to my young life, most especially my teen and early college years, being exhaustively given in an attempt to look one way for those whom I thought mattered to please while being another way by myself and with others whom I didn't think would notice or care. I desperately wanted my parents, my teachers, my coaches, my student pastor at church, and even most of my peers to think of me as a morally good guy who does the right thing. All of this while I secretly (or so I thought) would give myself over to my own desires, my selfish pride, and my sinful wishes. I had no problem with sinning in secret with things like pride, lust, alcohol, my thought life, and even with my motives, so long as, externally, I was still perceived as "good." I was a fraud but didn't know it or at least wouldn't admit it.

Over time I even grew more and more calloused to my sinful pattern of double living and I grew less and less concerned with the opinions and perceptions of others, so long as my sinful desires were being met and my personal pleasures were being satisfied. I was like the man that James describes in his New Testament letter: *"He is a double-minded man, unstable in all his ways"* (James 1:8 ESV). That was me, and, if I'm honest, at times still is ... double-minded and unstable. My life went this way throughout high school and for my first few years of college.

The summer before my junior year of college I was invited by a friend to join him in working on a cattle ranch in a small town in Colorado. The promise was terrible pay, but free room and board and most importantly, an adventure that few would be able to match. It seemed like an epic opportunity for a college kid. I talked to my parents and to Mary and everyone agreed it was worth a shot. In May of 1998, I left for Salida, Colorado, where I would begin working on the /LD ranch as a summer laborer. The owner of the /LD ranch was a semi-retired businessman from Austin, Texas, who had decided to move to Colorado and pursue his lifelong dream of ranching. In addition to being a cowboy and rancher, he was also a very strong Christian who used his ranch and summer employment opportunities as the means by which he could mentor and disciple young, college-age men, in the faith of God he enjoyed.

As it began, things were going along normally that summer. Work was hard, but the adventures were very cool. Some days the tasks were mundane and boring, but other days we would drive herds of cattle into the high country on horseback and be gone all day. Those trips were epic and hardly felt like work. We saw deer, elk, and all types of wildlife, all while sitting in the saddle and moving cows through what seemed like a hidden part of God's creation that had never been discovered before. The views were amazing, the weather was perfect, and the other college guys I worked with made the downtime fun.

The ranch owner had a structure for getting to know each of us college guys on a personal level. One day a week, each one of us would get up early for breakfast and Bible devotions with him. This was our one-on-one with this cowboy who loved Jesus so much, and it was his opportunity to personally and individually invest in us. Each meeting was an opportunity to share personally about our faith and to learn from this godly man. Sometimes, we would share; other times, he would tell us what his take was on a certain passage in the Bible and, if necessary, for him to challenge us on our beliefs and to give us food for our thoughts that day.

On one particular day, it was my turn for early morning devotions. I trudged down to the house from our trailer bunkhouse where we stayed, flopped down at the kitchen table, and prepared for another day of going through the spiritual motions. You see, I was a professional at faking my way through spiritual activities, like Bible study. Being so early, and being so full of myself, I was tired and I'm sure acting arrogantly that morning when out of nowhere, this ranch owner called me out. We were reading something in the Psalms, I still can't remember what, and I'm sure after giving some meaningless response to his question about what we were reading, this old cowboy went off on me. I don't remember everything he said verbatim, but the gist of it was this, "Connor, you're a primadonna!" (That word I absolutely remember.) "You're a jock who has always had a great deal of life handed to you on a silver platter. You're spoiled and I think you're a fake in regard to what you say you believe." Finally, he concluded with, "Son, I think you had better do some soul searching to find out if you're even a Christian and saved." What? I was furious! I quickly finished breakfast and started my workday early.

On this particular day, I had been given the task of spraying wild irises with an herbicide. I considered this the worst task on the ranch for a couple of reasons. First, this was a job done by yourself. You miss all of the fun of socializing and hanging out with the other guys on the ranch, which made the day go so much faster and made the work so much easier. Second, we did this work using a backpack sprayer and filled it with not only the water and chemical needed to kill the plants but with a blue dye so that you could tell what had been sprayed and what had not. (Now, if you're wondering why spraying wild irises would even be a job needed at a working cattle ranch, you're not alone. Essentially, while super boring to do, this work was necessary so that the invasive irises wouldn't overtake the pastures, ruining the native grasses and rendering the pasture useless for the much-needed grazing ground.) Finally, I hated this job mostly because the backpack sprayer leaked. So after a long, boring, isolated day of spraying plants in a pasture by yourself, you would go home to a back and backside that was stained with blue dye. Since it was a commercial dye, it wouldn't come off in just one or two showers either. Miserable.

Since it was a solo job and I was left out there all day with just my thoughts (and they weren't good) it turned out, I now know by God's grace, to be the perfectly timed task for me. I was stewing for what seemed like hours. I kept thinking, "How dare he challenge me and question my faith? Doesn't this guy know I was raised in a Christian home? I've been in church my whole life. I grew up in our church youth group. For the most part, I'm a good guy, and no one, certainly not this old man, knows about my secret sins!"

But the funny thing is, he didn't need to know about them. My double-minded life had led to an instability that I couldn't see. This cowboy knew I was "faking it" spiritually and, by God's grace, he had the courage to call me on it. Looking back on it today, I am so grateful for that cowboy's courage and boldness. It changed my life. In fact, while on a recent sabbatical back in the State of Colorado, I reflected that I have now celebrated over twenty spiritual birthdays as a Christian, since that tough breakfast conversation that summer.

Over the last several years I wondered what that man was up to and what he might think if he knew about what God has done with this "primadonna" since that summer in 1998. With Mary's encouragement, I looked him up, and within the last few years, we've connected. It has been really cool. I have had the opportunity to personally thank that brother in Christ for being willing to say something hard to a college kid who desperately needed to hear it.

So, there I was. Spraying wild irises in a pasture in the middle of a Colorado cattle ranch when I came face to face with my hypocrisy. Who was I? What did I believe? In whom did I trust? Was I truly saved? Those were the questions I couldn't escape that day. I wonder if there are any questions you can't escape. What about the questions I encouraged you to think about as I began this chapter?

Well, after a few hours of wrestling, I surrendered. On July 29, 1998, I prayed in the middle of that pasture and asked God to save me. I remember saying something like, "God, I'm tired of faking it. My life is a joke. I'm asking you for help. Please change me." And He did! Right then, right there, God saved me, and my life was transformed by His grace. Of course, while I am still a redemptive work in progress, I have never been the same since that day.

Now unfortunately after my salvation, I wasn't really discipled in my new-found faith and so I stayed in the shallow end of the gospel pool for several years. I still struggled with some of that old, besetting behavior, but being saved meant I now had God's Holy Spirit living within me to help guide me in my daily fight. The process was and is slow, but I began making gains and Jesus was slowly but surely becoming more and more the center of my life and the foundation upon which I lived it. I knew what it meant to struggle, I had known that my whole life. But now, in Christ, I knew what it meant to struggle well.

I began to live my life empowered by God's Spirit and to battle sin with integrity and hope. I was new. I was not made better. I had been made new. I knew what Paul meant when he wrote 2 Corinthians 5:17, *"Therefore, if anyone is in Christ, he is a new creation. The old has passed away; behold, the new has come"* (2 Corinthians 5:17 ESV). Today, I can say confidently that while I am not yet who I want to be, I am no longer who I was either. I'm changed by God's grace, saved!

Author Stephanie Hubach explains the gospel of Christ and the salvation of God in a way that I have only grown to appreciate more and more over these years since my conversion that summer day. She says, "The beauty of the gospel, if we truly understand it, is that each of us faces a complete barrier to participation in the kingdom of God due the profoundly disabled condition of our hearts. The good news is that Christ's perfect sacrifice applied to us makes our full participation in the life of God a reality."

After college and as a newlywed couple, Mary and I both knew we needed to find a good church to call home.

Fortunately, we found my home church from high school as the right fit for us to start. We quickly settled in and made friends with other young couples. We found a great small group in our Sunday school class of other young marrieds and our teachers, who were our parent's age, proved to be incredible godly mentors in our life. This was a truly sweet season for us as a couple. We grew closer to Jesus and Jesus grew us closer to one another.

In our church, my high school student pastor was still serving there at that time and after only a year or so of us attending, he asked me to lead the eighth-grade boys in Bible study. I reluctantly said yes and within a few months fell in love with those guys and the ministry we were having together. After getting them through that year, and before beginning their freshman year of high school, the girls of the same grade were now in need of a teacher, so I convinced Mary to join me and together we took that group of students from their freshman year through their graduation. It was a great time of fun and deep spiritual growth for both Mary and me.

It's a funny thing, as you study and work to teach God's Word to others, God has a gracious way of teaching His Word to you. This was certainly the case for me. I was growing in my faith faster than any other time in my life and I was falling more in love with Jesus and His Church. During this season, our student pastor left the church and the weekly responsibilities to lead the student ministry fell to Mary and me as the short-term solution of sorts. We worked to plan the Wednesday night worship gatherings, the Sunday morning Bible studies, and any student ministry events that came each semester as well.

On one Wednesday night, we had invited a guest speaker to come and minister to the students. While sitting in the crowd and listening to what he said, I heard God speak to me in, what was at the time, the most clear I had ever heard His voice before. God said, "Connor, you sell your business because I've called you to this." Well, as you might expect, I responded as every mature Christian should, I panicked. I didn't tell Mary anything and was working diligently to convince myself that I was making the whole thing up and I hadn't actually heard what I thought.

That following Sunday the pastor preached a sermon and to this day I'm convinced he was speaking only to me. The Holy Spirit was all over me and He was asking me, "Are you going to say something about what I've told you or not?" As we headed home from church, with our three-year-old and six-month-old in their car seats, driving to our big home with the pool, I looked over and told Mary with tears streaming down my face, "I think God is calling me into the ministry." Mary's first response was, "Maybe you're just supposed to volunteer more." Ha! I kind of hoped at that time that she was right. But very quickly, as the calling God gave me and the feeling He instilled in me only grew stronger, Mary agreed. Honestly, Mary jumped on board with this left turn in our "charmed" life right away. She said she wasn't surprised by this revelation and from the moment God made this calling clear, I have always had her full support.

Within a few weeks of this radical calling God gave me, I met with our pastor who affirmed God's Word to me and shared Mary's view that this shift was not a surprise to him. My family likewise affirmed God's Word to me and shared the opinion that they had seen God's growth of me over the last several years and could see the shape of ministry being formed in my life. So, I surrendered.

God called this landscape business owner to pursue vocational ministry, by serving His Church. I wasn't sure what that meant, but I was convinced it was what I was supposed to do. So, I surrendered.

Not long after this calling and conviction came, I was driving around Dallas one day, between sales appointments and job inspections for my landscape company, and I was listening to a popular radio program hosted by Dave Ramsey, the financial wizard who helps hundreds of thousands of families get out of debt and enjoy financial freedom instead. I liked the program because I thought Dave was entertaining, I appreciated his financial principles, I knew he was a Christian and I loved hearing people give their "debt-free" screams on his show. Plus, if I'm being honest, I listened to sports talk radio the rest of the time in the car and this felt like a semi-redemptive way to justify that.

Since one left turn (my calling into the ministry) wasn't enough, I again heard God tell me, although admittedly not in the audible way I felt before, our family was to sell our big home and to pay off all our debt. When I shared THIS news with Mary, the shock wasn't as severe. After all, this made sense practically as we knew there would likely be a significant shift in our income whenever we started our first ministry position. Additionally, we knew we could use the excess cash flow to assist in paying for seminary if I was going to pursue the education that would accompany my calling.

As it turned out, the debt-free move was the right one. We would certainly need to free up money for some changes in our family's expenses, and it would be for a new ministry that God would entrust only to us. It is just not the ministry that I expected. In fact, it is a life and a ministry so much bigger than that...

Before this chapter concludes, I want to offer some clarity to my conversation about Jesus, salvation, and sin. If you are wondering what salvation is or what being saved means, let me just quickly explain. The Bible teaches, and if we are being honest we all know as well, that we are ALL sinners. Every one of us. Sin is common to all. In fact, the Bible frames it this way, *"For all have sinned and fall short of the glory of God"* (Romans 3:23 ESV). Now, I would define sin as our choosing to rebel against God's design for all things. As an example, the Bible teaches that God designed sex to be enjoyed and stewarded in a covenant marriage between one man and one woman. However, when we experience sex in any means outside of or other than that, we have committed sin. And the same could be said of how we treat food or live-in relationships or handling money or use our minds. God has a design for how we operate with or steward all of it. Any use outside of His good design is our choosing to rebel against Him and the Bible calls this sin.

The effects of sin are both in us and all around us. Just think about your actions within the last week or turn on the news for proof of what I'm talking about. Because sin exists, it has damaged or broken the perfect creation that God first made as good. The creation of God, as recorded in the Bible, words the "goodness" of the creation this way, *"And God saw everything that he had made, and behold, it was very good. And there was evening and there was morning, the sixth day"* (Genesis 1:31 ESV).

Now, as sinners, we are separated from God who is infinitely perfect and entirely holy. He is not like us in that God has no sin. Because we are sinful, we cannot overcome our separation on our own and something must be done to restore us back to God. The Bible teaches that the wages of sin is death. In other words, what we owe God, as the just payment for our sin, is death. But, as sinners who cannot pay this debt on our own, God miraculously and graciously gives us life instead and reconciles us back to Himself by taking our punishment for us. Listen to how this is described in God's Word, *"For the wages of sin is death, but the free gift of God is eternal life in Christ Jesus our Lord"* (Romans 6:23 ESV). Crazy right?

What's more, and what I lived the first twenty-one years of my life with no true understanding of, is that God doesn't wait for us to clean ourselves up or stop committing our sin or change our lives before He decides to graciously give Himself as the payment of death that is owed for our sin. In fact, the Bible teaches that it is in the midst of our brokenness from sin that Jesus, God's only Son, who is God Himself, came to earth, died in our place and for our sins. *"But God shows his love for us in that while we were still sinners, Christ died for us"* (Romans 5:8 ESV). This is THE good news for us! God isn't waiting on us to change, He's waiting on us to surrender so that He can change us. God hasn't withheld His forgiveness because we're not good enough, we haven't yet received it only when we're not yet convinced of our need for it.

Finally, the Bible teaches that God's forgiveness and our reconciliation back to Him is available when we confess that Jesus is our only hope and when we believe that He is God who died our death and has risen for our eternal life. Salvation comes when we truly believe that He alone can actually save us. Listen to the beauty of this reality from God's Word, *"Because, if you confess with your mouth that Jesus is Lord and believe in your heart that God raised him from the dead, you will be saved. For with the heart one believes and is justified, and with the mouth one confesses and is saved"* (Romans 10:9–10 ESV). Confession is the recognition and acknowledgment of something that a person believes to be true. Belief is the giving of your highest trust to something or in this case, someone who you can't entirely explain or fully understand. That's why a Christian's relationship with God is founded on faith. Two of my favorite passages that highlight this truth are found in Hebrews, *"Now faith is the assurance of things hoped for, the conviction of things not seen"* (Hebrews 11:1 ESV). And in Paul's letter to the Ephesian church, *"For by grace you have been saved through faith. And this is not your own doing; it is the gift of God, not a result of works, so that no one may boast"* (Ephesians 2:8–9 ESV).

Ultimately, what I believe makes God's gift of salvation so life-changing is that just as everyone is a sinner, likewise, salvation is made available to everyone who believes in God for the forgiveness for it. Please be encouraged by this powerful truth from God's Word, *"For everyone who calls on the name of the Lord will be saved"* (Romans 10:13 ESV). EVERYONE who calls on God, as I did in that cow pasture in the summer of 1998, and asks Him to help, save, rescue, and restore will be saved. Everyone. Anyone. I am absolutely convinced, by my own story if nothing else, that no one is beyond the grace and mercy and forgiveness of our great God. No one!

It is likely that, if you are reading this book, you have experienced some suffering in your life, and in some ways, it can be a challenge to reconcile that experience which is bad, with the gift of God's salvation, which is good. I get that. I would simply share with you an encouraging reminder from author Randy Alcorn about this. "Whenever you feel tempted to ask God, 'Why did you do this *to* me?' Look at the Cross and ask, 'Why did you do that *for* me?'" [6]

Friend, God loves you! He has given His Son, Jesus, for you. Jesus lived the life we could never live and yet He died the death that we certainly deserve. He did this so that, if we place our faith in Him, we might be saved! That is the Gospel. That is the good news of God. That's all that it is and that is everything that it is. Jesus and His Gospel changed my life. He is still changing my life. Has He changed yours?

Chapter 4

"CHANGED"

Once Mary and I sold our home and paid off our debt, we moved into an apartment with our two small children (Kathryn and Coleman) and began restructuring our budget, saving as much as possible. We began setting money aside to make a down payment on a smaller, more affordable home, in preparation for what we knew would be a change in income that accompanied the change in vocation.

This was a sweet season for us. Mary and I have commented to one another many times since then, that with the simplicity of our life, and being convinced that we were in the center of God's will, being unusually obedient to what He had called us to do, it was just a great time for our young family to grow. And we did grow. We were flourishing, in all of the ways that matter: spiritually, personally, relationally, and emotionally. Of course, as I stated before, God was preparing us for ministry. It just wasn't the ministry we had thought.

Mary and I knew we wanted to have a large family. So, by God's grace, we got pregnant and were expecting our third child, a little girl. Mary was due in November of 2008, which was excellent for a few reasons. First, the timing of our daughter's arrival would allow us to make housing adjustments and get settled into a new place before Christmas and the craziness of the holidays with a newborn. Second, Mary wouldn't be miserably pregnant in the most miserable months of a Texas summer.

God was so good to us. Our "charmed" life was continuing to take shape. It wasn't exactly what we had dreamed up before, but this change in our family by my vocational calling into the ministry hadn't derailed the idyllic narrative we were writing for ourselves on our journey.

Once we found out we were having a little girl, Mary and I settled on the name Elizabeth Faye Bales, but we decided from the beginning that we would always call her "Libby" for short. Mary's pregnancy was perfect. She had no complications, things were smooth sailing (says the guy who wasn't carrying the baby), and like prior pregnancies, things moved along without any surprises or concerns along the way.

October 6, 2008, was a Monday. Mary was about five weeks away from her due date, something she had met with each of our two children before. I remember the morning perfectly. I had hung around the house a little later that day because Mary was trying to get things together and was making final preparations for Libby's baby nursery. We had stored a few things (i.e., bassinet, baby bouncy chair, and play saucer) in the attic, and Mary needed me to get them down for her to clean up and make ready for Libby's arrival in a few weeks. While I was in the attic, Mary came to the bottom of the stairs to tell me she wasn't feeling right and she thought she might be starting labor. I tried to keep calm, reminding her it was too early for labor, and so I casually dismissed her concerns by chalking it up to Braxton-Hicks, false contractions. In an abundance of caution, we agreed she should call the doctor and let him determine the next steps that day.

Mary's doctor insisted she stop by his office for a quick check and so I adjusted my schedule that morning and we went in for Mary to be seen, and I assumed sent home. The doctor informed us after a few minutes that Mary was in fact in labor and we went directly from his office to the labor-and-delivery floor of the hospital next door.

At 5:25 p.m., our daughter Libby burst onto the scene, weighing six pounds two ounces She had bleached white-blonde hair, an absolute toe-head. And a tiny one to boot. Now, other than the unusually blonde hair, the only thing that physically stuck out to Mary and me at Libby's birth was that both of her feet were severely malformed, in that they were pointing straight out to the side and straight up, almost touching the sides of her little legs. They were, "funky feet," as we would learn to call them. The doctor, however, noticing our faces of concern and hearing our (my) repeated questions about her feet, explained the anomaly as possibly being the result of positioning in the womb and assured us that we shouldn't be worried, that we would know a lot more in the days ahead.

But, we (I) were worried. Normally, at least with our older two children, after Mary had given birth, the doctors would deliver the baby, hand the baby to nursing staff in the room who would clean the baby and immediately check on the baby for obvious concerns, and then very quickly hand the baby right back to Mary for some precious bonding time together. With Libby, the doctor delivered her, and the nurses began checking her and cleaning her. After a few minutes, more and more staff began entering the room and ultimately they just took her away. We were so confused. Something was obviously wrong, but no one was saying anything except mostly to one another as it related to working on Libby. All Mary and I knew was they never gave Libby back.

The doctor continued to tend to Mary, while a nurse informed me that Libby wasn't breathing as well as they wanted and so they would take her to the Neonatal Intensive Care Unit, so that they could give her more attention and if needed supplement her oxygen some, to help her get caught up. The explanation didn't sound too bad and the nurse didn't seem that alarmed, so I stayed with Mary and began making phone calls to let family and friends know that Libby had shown up early. After a few hours, a neonatologist came by our room to let us know that Libby was stable, and that I was welcome to come down and see her, but that they had detected a heart murmur and, tomorrow, a pediatric cardiologist would be coming to the hospital to examine Libby and they would conduct an echocardiogram to try to determine the reason for the murmur so a diagnosis could be given.

We thanked the doctor for his time and attention to our little girl and told him we would be anxiously awaiting tomorrow's appointment with the cardiologist to find out exactly what was wrong. Mary and I then, together, went down to the NICU to see our Libby, to touch her, love on her, and to meet those incredible nurses who would be tending to her so closely. After spending some much needed time with Libby, we headed back to our room so that Mary could rest, but honestly, because of the surprise of Libby's early arrival, the complications of her delivery, and the news of the heart murmur and tomorrow's pending appointment, neither of us slept much that night. Obviously, we were excited about Libby's arrival, but we were also very concerned about what little we already knew that wasn't quite right.

The next day we met with the pediatric cardiologist who examined Libby and we were informed that Libby had a fairly severe congenital heart defect called Tetralogy of Fallot. Essentially, this particular defect has four parts of the heart that are affected by the abnormality. It is unusual, but not entirely uncommon, and fortunately, the doctor told us that with the advancements of medicine and surgical procedures, Libby's defect could be surgically repaired and that we should expect a first surgery to be sometime around her first birthday. Now, writing this today, years later, I recognize what a blessing it is to have modern medicine that allows my daughter's heart defect to be surgically repaired, but then, on that day, I (we) was crushed knowing that she would require any surgery at all. In an instant, it seemed like everything changed.

Libby stayed in the NICU for eleven days. Mary and I went to see her twice every day. Mary was trying to provide milk for the nurses to feed to Libby and we wanted to spend as much time with her as we could. Libby grew stronger, more stable and once she gained enough weight that we could be cleared to load her safely into a baby carrier, we were sent home to begin our new life with this fragile little girl.

On the way home from the hospital, the day of Libby's discharge, we went directly to our pediatrician's office for Libby's first visit. We spent a long time with our doctors. Although we didn't know them well, they proved to be an unbelievable gift from God to our family. They are an incredible husband-and-wife team who took such good care of us for so many years. On that day, they got up to speed on Libby's heart condition, heard our plan regarding her feet being fixed, and then they told us what regular well-checks and weight checks needed to look like going forward. This then started for us a "new normal" of sorts. Libby began seeing a pediatric cardiologist every week for heart checks and then our pediatricians every week for weight checks, and they would communicate between their offices to make sure that progress was being made where it needed to be and that conditions weren't worsening at the same time. Things had certainly changed for us.

At one of our first visits with the cardiologist in his office, he told us that Libby's defective valve was leaking quite a bit and surgery might not be in a year, but perhaps closer to nine months. Within a week or two after that, he said six months was more likely. Only a week or two later, he informed us that the leak was continuing to worsen and changed her surgery date to three months and at the next appointment after that, we scheduled the surgery for Monday, December 15, 2008.

I'll never forget that day. I got up early with Kathryn and Coleman and took them to Krispy Kreme Donuts as a treat that morning before Mary and I had to have Libby at the hospital for pre-op. I knew we wouldn't see the older kids much in the days ahead and I wanted to have some time to spoil them a little before the chaos began. I remember I was so nervous. I ate one donut and threw that up in the parking lot immediately after buckling the kids into their car seats. I should've known something was really wrong. Who wastes the greatness of a warm Krispy Kreme donut by throwing it up?

Mary was a lot tougher than me, at least on the outside. We took Libby in that day and after leaving her with the anesthesiologist and heading into the surgical waiting room, which by God's grace again, was filled with family and friends, we endured what was one of the longest days of our lives. Mary, as it turns out, clenches her jaw when she's nervous and upset. So, she developed ulcers in the mouth days after Libby's surgery was complete. I don't hide my nerves as well, so I spent about every hour or two crying and vomiting in the men's room for most of that day.

We were the picture of stability, let me tell you. And … we were a long way from the "charmed" life that I had dreamt of so many years before. But yet again, God's grace was overwhelmingly good to us as Libby's heart repair was a complete success and she recovered more quickly postoperatively than the doctors had even expected her to. We were thrilled.

In a seemingly insignificant conversation with us one day, while Libby was still recovering from surgery in the hospital, one doctor recommended that Libby have labs drawn to check for any genetic abnormalities, as some are linked to her particular heart condition and we certainly had enough reason for the tests to be run. This seemed like an excellent idea to us, after all, I knew that once we had her heart repaired and we could get her feet in some braces and get those fixed as well, it would be smooth sailing for our girl and our family could get back to our version of normal.

In early January of 2009, a geneticist called us to let us know that the results of Libby's genetics testing had returned and that she would like to meet with us to go over the findings. I think instinctively, Mary and I both knew that meant they had found something but given our lack of knowledge regarding anything related to the science of genetics and our confidence that we had already hurdled the largest obstacle in Libby's life with a successful heart surgery, we headed into this appointment without knowing what we should expect.

On Thursday, January 15, 2009, our geneticist informed us that Libby had an extremely rare genetic abnormality called Trisomy 16p. Specifically, Libby was born with a partial translocation of her sixteenth chromosome. This particular genetic abnormality is so rare because, as our geneticist told us, it is "incompatible with life." We were told that Libby's particular anomaly was only known to have been found in about thirty other people at that time (Naturally, any one of you curiosity seekers reading this book is going to try to Google this diagnosis of Trisomy 16p, and there is a chance you will find something, but not much. Because there isn't much. It's rare. Certainly, there must be more cases of this particular genetic abnormality, but most are likely untested or those who have it don't live long enough to be tested, and therefore they go undiagnosed. So, the rarity of our Libby's condition is extreme.).

I remember asking the doctor, "Is this like Downs Syndrome?" which was literally the only thing I knew in my limited understanding of genetic defects. The doctor simply responded, "Oh, Mr. Bales, this is so much more severe. I would tell you that if you hadn't already had your daughter's heart repaired, I might have counseled you against it."

So, as you might imagine, trying to soak in this news ... Mary and I were undone. Everything had changed yet again! We were wrecked. Devastated doesn't even begin to describe our feelings.

One of the last things the doctor told us was: "Fifty percent of children born with a genetic abnormality this severe die in their infancy. Libby would most likely not live to see her second birthday, and you should go home and make her comfortable and enjoy what little time you have left." This was soul-crushing.

Our daughter was diagnosed with very severe, life-threatening, life-altering, special needs. I still get emotional just thinking about that day. I can remember the doctor's office, the colors on the wall, the furniture where we sat. I can remember the medical book the doctor showed us with the one picture of a young man with Trisomy 16 and the one page dedicated to Libby's condition.

Author and special needs parent Stephanie Hubach shares this reality for a mom and dad perfectly when she writes, "Parents whose child has been diagnosed with a disability experience the sense of a *loss of expectations*— and the associated grief that comes with having a child who is markedly different from the one whom they had anticipated. This does not imply that the parents won't love the child who *has* entered their lives. Indeed, they may eventually find their capacity to love expanded beyond their wildest expectations. However, there will be a significant grief that needs to be experienced even as they attempt to fully embrace the child who has arrived. Over the years, this sense of loss will often be revisited when typical milestones in a child's life are encountered under altered circumstances for *this* child. These milestones may include birthdays, graduations, going off to college, and other rites of passage." [7]

I didn't understand. I didn't have a category for this. My hurt was so deep, and my sadness was so real that my chest ached. I remember leaving the doctor's office and heading back to work to gather my things so that I could meet Mary back at home. And, to my shame to this day, I let Mary and Libby ride home after that appointment alone. When we got home, we hugged and cried and cried and cried. We called our families, and I'll never forget that both of my brothers, Jayson and Neil, immediately rushed over to the house that afternoon to spend time with us and make sure we were okay. But we were not. I was numb. Mary was numb.

This diagnosis of devastation felt like it was too much for us to bear. Life had changed for us. We were changed…

Chapter 5

"CONFUSED"

I mentioned in the introduction to the book that being a Texan, I am used to strange weather. In fact, the disparity in weather across the expanse of our state is something that is almost celebrated, in an unusual way. And although it is not unusual, and certainly not limited to Texas, I'm always struck by the limiting way foggy weather can affect a person's routine, simply by limiting vision and creating confusion as it's being navigated. When we received Libby's diagnosis, it felt like a dense fog settled into my mind. As it related to Libby's challenges, the only thing I had any certainty about was that Mary and I were going to love her with everything we had and that we would do anything and everything in our power to give her the best life with every opportunity we could afford. Other than that, I was foggy. I wasn't thinking clearly, I wasn't praying clearly, I wasn't leading clearly, I probably wasn't even loving clearly. With all of the emotions we faced, a dense fog had set in on us and it was affecting how we navigated our life.

In the days and weeks after Libby's diagnosis, Mary and I began to digest our new reality. In the mental processing, a crazy-wide range of emotions flooded us—that fog I mentioned a moment ago. We felt shocked, saddened, angry, disappointed, hurt, disgusted, terrified, and broken-hearted … just to name a few. Perhaps the emotion or feeling which surprised me the most, and yet hung around me what felt like all of the time, was the confusion. Now, I would like to tell you that because of my relationship with God through Jesus, and the blessing I enjoyed of God's Holy Spirit alive inside me, that I handled all of these emotions with incredible maturity and spiritual integrity that is worthy of a New Testament story. That, however, would not be true. Not even close.

I could not reconcile in my mind the "Why" behind the "What" in Libby's diagnosis and our family's story. Perhaps because of my background in landscape architecture and my traditionally linear pattern of thinking, I just truly did not understand how God could let this happen to my daughter. I could not understand why God would let this happen to our little girl. I was confused. I was thoroughly perplexed. And my confusion led to more frustration and that frustration led to greater confusion and the cycle was getting worse. I felt like a road warrior who has set out on a journey, only to be limited to a stop or a slow crawl because a dense fog has hindered him from knowing the direction to go and what he should be looking for all along the way.

I kept hoping the fog would burn off, like it does most often when it is a part of an early morning weather pattern here in Texas. Mary and I attempted to settle into our new rhythm in our life with Libby. This included a steady stream of doctor's appointments and therapies, a substantial regimen of medicines, the consistency of insurance battles one after another, and thousands and thousands of dollars spent trying our best to find the best care for our little girl. It was (and is) exhausting and I don't know that I had the depth, maturity, or wisdom to process this new life and all of its new experiences which created these new emotions very well at all. In hindsight, I now know that my struggle, my confusion, my fog, was essentially me wrestling with the sovereignty and goodness of God. I'll explain more of what I have discovered later in the book, but my confusion was quite simply my lack of understanding of the cause and effect nature of life in our broken world. After all, if you'll remember, so much of my life was "charmed." I hadn't had to truly reconcile much in the way of brokenness until life with Libby forced that reality upon us in the most serious ways.

Paul Tripp summarizes the root of my confusion and frustration when he writes, "Your suffering is more powerfully shaped by what's in your heart than by what's in your body or in the world around you." In other words, the external pressure of my life and our circumstances simply served to reveal an internal problem rooted within me. Tripp goes on to say, "Your responses to the situations in your life, whether physical, relational, or circumstantial, are always more determined by what is inside you (your heart) than by the things you are facing. This is why people have dramatically different responses to the same situations of difficulty. This is why the writer of Proverbs says: *'Keep your heart with all vigilance, for from it flow the springs of life.* (Proverbs 4:23 ESV).'" [8]

I take comfort knowing that I'm not alone in my lack of understanding of the cause-and-effect nature of our broken world. To that, I've discovered a prominent story recorded in the Bible in which the disciples of Jesus were attempting to reconcile the exact same thing. In this particular story, the disciples don't have a personal relationship with the person experiencing the unexplained suffering, like Mary and I do with Libby, but their confusion as to the cause and effect surrounding it is the same as ours. Listen to this story recorded in John, Chapter 9: *"As he passed by, he saw a man blind from birth. And his disciples asked him, 'Rabbi, who sinned, this man or his parents, that he was born blind?'"* (John 9:1–2 ESV). Now to me, it seems very reasonable, for the disciples to have this question about the cause for this man's blindness. In fact, although we don't know how the writer knew it, he includes the detail that this particular man had suffered his condition of blindness from birth. So that left a very difficult cause and effect question in the disciples' minds as they (like me) attempted to reconcile the "Why" behind this "What."

After all, if this man had lost his vision after suffering a tragic accident at work, or if his blindness had been the understandable result of a disease he had suffered from as a child, then logically there would be a reasonable, explainable cause which yielded this effect of blindness. But, that's not what our story says is what happened. This man was born blind. Like Libby, there was nothing that seemed to cause this suffering. Mary had nothing unusual about her pregnancy and there were no accidents while Libby was in utero. Likewise, other than showing up a little earlier than expected, there were no complications with Libby's delivery. This reality of our story, and the story of the blind man in John 9, left the disciples of Jesus and me confused.

Now, I will say that theologically, the question of cause and effect in this Bible story is a very understandable one for the disciples to have. These men were just average first-century Jews whose very world has been turned upside down by the life and teaching of Jesus. For them, the idea of pain, suffering, and evil were explained away by associating those things as consequences of sin. In other words, if someone was suffering from some ailment, dire circumstance, or severe problem, the reasons for this would have been understood as having something to do with that person's failures. As did most Palestinian Jews of their day, they linked sin and suffering together. And in one sense, they were absolutely correct to do so. You see, as I outlined briefly in Chapter Two, when God created the world and everything in it, the Bible says it was "very good." In fact, it was perfect as God had designed it. It was a created world without sin and therefore without the consequences of sin, which would most certainly include suffering. But, because of the rebellion of our first parents, Adam and Eve, all humanity has subsequently suffered the consequences of sin's fracturing all that God had made. The result is that our world is broken. We are broken. And while sometimes the brokenness shows up in creation through natural disasters or in the created through acts of evil and terror. It also shows up on the creation through illness and human suffering. Sometimes it is blindness from birth, or it could be Trisomy 16p. The problem in this story is that the disciples are trying to connect the sin condition of the entire human race with the specific suffering of this individual born blind. And they can't reconcile who is to blame or what is the cause, which rendered this effect. And, if I'm being honest, this is something I can very closely relate to myself.

My questions were, "God, why my daughter? She's innocent. Have you not seen what she's going through? She's suffering. Look at what has been done to her little body already. Look at the medicines she's constantly having to take. Look ahead toward the future she's being told she won't have. God, why our family? We're doing the right things and trying to follow you. We're being generous with our money and our time and we are faithfully serving your Church." And, although I'm embarrassed to say it now, I even thought, "God, I'm in seminary! I have surrendered my life to a calling into the ministry." I was literally giving God a resume of reasons why the cause of Libby's suffering did not match the effect. Yes, I was confused. I was foggy and could not get the weather to break.

I just could not understand the reason for Libby's suffering. I was confused and I was also very angry. My self-righteousness mixed with my fear and mixed with my grief was the perfect cocktail for this theological and personal conundrum, which I couldn't reconcile in my mind. I remember thinking very clearly that I could bear it if this suffering was mine. I'm a big boy, a tough guy. I can wrap my mind around my own hardship, but I couldn't understand it being her. My little Libby was innocent. She had done nothing to deserve what she was dealing with, and yet I was watching her suffer very seriously. I couldn't reconcile the cause and effect of this, and it wrecked me.

Again, Tripp summarizes my struggle personally when he writes, "Because our complaints are rooted not just in horizontal dissatisfaction (with people and situations), but also in vertical disappointment (with God), discouragement has the potential to become spiritually debilitating. We don't sufficiently consider the effect that complaint has on us and the way we think about and respond to our relationship with God." [9]

The disciples must have been wondering the same things. For them, they needed some clarity from Jesus as to the "Why" of this man born blind that led to his "What." I don't think they were wrecked by the condition of this blind man like I was about Libby, but they were curious to be sure and I'm guessing empathetic as well, given the ministry mindedness they most certainly had learned from Jesus Himself by now. They were trying to work out one of those ideas that we spoke about earlier. It appears that up to this point the disciples, and perhaps most everyone else in that culture, had assumed that human suffering was a consequence of personal or familial sin. They tried to explain away the unexplainable. Haven't we done that? Haven't we all tried to understand the reason for suffering? I've already admitted that I have. I attempted to offer a litany of reasons why it made no sense for Libby to be suffering as she was and for the Bales family to be enduring the hardship that came along with it. And that questioning, brought on by the fog of emotion, is what is going on here. In this passage, we see that clearly, the dilemma we have all thought or wondered aloud, the disciples boldly voiced. The disciples sought an explanation as to what unmerited human suffering could be attributed to, at its origin. I understand why they asked, and I appreciate the vulnerability that it must have taken for them to acknowledge the need to learn here.

In their book, *Why O' God?*, authors Larry Waters and Roy Zuck build on this dilemma the disciples were facing:

"This thought has crossed our minds many times. *What did we do? Is there some sin we have not confessed? Is there something God is punishing us for?* We have searched our hearts. Jesus's answer is comforting. 'It was not that this man sinned, or his parents, but that the works of God might be displayed in him' (v.3). Sometimes we sound like Job asking the questions God never intends to answer this side of heaven. But we are thankful that while we may not have the answers, he does give us a purpose. His glory." [10] However, I have known very personally the question the disciples were only asking theoretically.

How about you? Have you ever experienced the fog of emotional confusion? Perhaps some of you reading this book right now are attempting to navigate your own journey of suffering or disappointment or failure, only to be stranded by the dense fog of confusion, hindering your rational ability to navigate the journey you are on right now. It probably feels like the fog is so thick, you can't see to get down the road. I get it. I really, really get it. Maybe, like the disciples and me, you also have questioned or are now questioning the "Why" behind your "What." I get that too. While I won't attempt to try and talk you out of your emotions, I wouldn't dare. I think you are entitled to most of the emotions that accompany suffering and hardship, and I also believe that they are often a necessary part of the process for navigating a healthy way forward. I would, however, be remiss if I didn't remind you of what the Bible makes very clear. God gave us our emotions, and therefore He can handle our sharing these emotions with Him.

Randy Alcorn encourages honesty with God as he reminds us of Job's story of suffering. "The Bible models honesty with God concerning the problem of evil and suffering. Job candidly expressed his doubts as he questioned God about his suffering: "I will not keep silent; I will speak out in the anguish of my spirit, I will complain in the bitterness of my soul ... I despise my life ... If I have sinned, what have I done to you, O watcher of men? Why have you made me your target? Have I become a burden to you?" (Job 7:11, 16, 20). Just as God knew exactly how Job felt before he said a word, so God knows how you feel and what you're thinking. You can't hide it, so don't bother trying. When you pretend you don't feel hurt or angry or devastated, you're not fooling God. Be honest! Naomi cried, "The Almighty has made my life very bitter" (Ruth 1:20). David asked God, "Why have you forsaken me?" (Psalm 22:1). Jesus repeated the same question on the cross. Don't misunderstand; I am *not* encouraging you to be angry at God or to blame Him. He deserves no blame. Rather, I am encouraging you to honestly confess to God your feelings of hurt, resentment, and anger." [11]

Honesty with God is the best way forward. He is the safest outlet and audience we have. In fact, I would plead with you to process ALL of your emotions with God. Tell Him you are angry, sad, broken-hearted, grieved, frustrated, afraid, and confused. He can handle it, and even more than that, He wants us to share them with Him.

In his book *God's Grace in Your Suffering*, author David Powlison talks about this subject of honesty with God this way, "Seek the Lord honestly. In turning toward him, you will likely be turning away from instinctive and habitual sins. Anxiety? Anger? Despair? Escapism? He is merciful. He 'opposes the proud but gives grace to the humble' (James 4:6). Don't be afraid to tell the Lord the truth about your sufferings, your sins, your desires for mercy, your struggles. Dozens of Psalms have walked that road. Ask your Father to give you His Holy Spirit. All wisdom, trust, peace, courage, love, endurance, and hope are the fruit of His personal touch. Honest wrestling is not magic. It's not 'claiming the victory.' It's not finding a religious truism to short-circuit the process. And it's not wallowing in heartache and self-pity. God is taking us in His direction. Ask. Seek. Knock. He found you first and he is willing to be found." [12]

When Hannah was angry and upset because she could not conceive and have a child, the Bible says she took those emotions to God. *"She was deeply distressed and prayed to the LORD and wept bitterly"* (1 Samuel 1:10 ESV). Peter told the persecuted first-century Church to bring their angst and worry to God. *"Casting all your anxieties on him, because he cares for you"* (1 Peter 5:7 ESV). King David, when facing fear in his life, took them directly to God in prayer. *"I sought the LORD, and he answered me and delivered me from all my fears"* (Psalm 34:4 ESV). When Jesus faced His most distressing moments on earth, in preparation for His death on a cross, He prayed to God and shared all His emotion. *"Then Jesus went with them to a place called Gethsemane, and he said to his disciples, 'Sit here, while I go over there and pray.' And taking with him Peter and the two sons of Zebedee, he began to be sorrowful and troubled. Then he said to them, 'My soul is very sorrowful, even to death; remain here, and watch with me.' And going a little farther he fell on his face and prayed, saying, 'My Father, if it be possible, let this cup pass from me; nevertheless, not as I will, but as you will.'"* (Matthew 26:36–39 ESV).

In his book, *Dark Clouds Deep Mercy,* author Mark Vroegop gives a very honest explanation of these emotions or laments. "Complaint gives voice to our hard questions. Life is filled with a variety of suffering. Pain comes in many forms. Lament speaks into all the sorrows of life— no matter how small or big. Sorrow could enter your life because of unfulfilled longings, loneliness, an ailing body, or an unfair supervisor at work. It could come in the form of job loss, financial struggles, a broken engagement, or ongoing conflict in a marriage. Our hearts can groan under the weight of infertility, cancer, a failed adoption, an adulterous spouse, or wayward children. The longer we live, the more pain we see. God could intervene, but there are times—many times—when he chooses not to. That's the tension of complaint." [13]

So, if you find yourself facing the fog of emotion and confusion, you're not alone. And if you aren't sure what to do with these emotions, and you don't know how to clear the fog, follow the pattern of these brothers and sisters from the Bible. Follow the pattern of Jesus. Give these emotions to God. Process these feelings, all of these questions, with Him. He can handle it. All of it. Our God controls the weather; the winds and waves obey Him. He will burn the fog away.

Chapter 6
"CALM"

People always talk about the calm before the storm, and, indeed, many times prior to a severe weather event, if you go outside and look around and listen, you will sense an eerie calmness just before the storm hits. Before the thunder cracks and the lightning flashes and the trees are bent sideways by the fury of a major storm, there can be calm. Sometimes, the calm might include blue skies and there seems to be no wind and there is a clarity in the air that makes it feel totally strange. But there is also a calm *after* the storm. This calm doesn't get talked about much. I think it is usually ignored because everyone is so busy attempting to assess the damage from the storm, but it is a pleasant calmness just the same. Now, you don't usually have to look far to see the after-effects of the storm. Sometimes debris is strewn about, power might have been knocked out or, occasionally, even buildings and houses have visible damage from the storm. But the weather is usually calm. The sun is often bright. The wind settles into a breeze and actually serves to circulate the smell of clean air after a needed, cleansing rain. After Libby's storm had hit and we had finished assessing all of the damage, the Bales family enjoyed a wonderful season of calm. Oh, the effects of the storm were visible to anyone paying attention, but the weather of our lives had calmed way down.

Mary and I have grown fond of using the term "new normal" to describe our life after Libby. Of course, as we've grown and had more challenges and more of life's curveballs thrown our way, we have since discovered that eventually everyone has a "new normal" and that every time life demands a massive change or a major adjustment or a significant loss, a "new normal" is what every person adjusts to thereafter. And so it was for us. Once we got through heart surgery and began to get some sense of "normalcy" to our family's rhythm, things started to settle into a routine and our family began to adjust to what this new life and these new challenges would bring. (I use that word in quotes as I know there is no such thing as "normal" and that everything is subjective based on each person's individual perspective ... but you get the idea.)

With our older two children, Mary and I were pretty regimented about sleeping patterns and behavior. We had both kids in our room in bassinets until about six or eight weeks old and then we moved them into their own room and into their cribs and we maintained this schedule with consistency, despite some of the hurdles that come with helping a newborn baby adjust to change. With Libby, however, all the rules went out the window. Libby slept in a bassinet in our room, followed by a pack-n-play in our room until she was about eighteen months old. Mary and I were so concerned with her medical fragility and had been so conditioned to see that we avoided any additional complications, that we simply adjusted to this rhythm and made it work.

And it did. It worked.

Libby began to gain weight after heart surgery, something that she was unable to do prior. We began seeing specialists about Libby's developmental delays, her physical disabilities, and of course stayed on top of her medical frailty with her pediatric team. Libby was doing very well. To the average person, when Libby was a baby you wouldn't have known anything was wrong. She did what all babies do. But, as Libby got older, her delays became more noticeable and she began to miss milestones which, because of what the doctors had told us to expect, wasn't necessarily a surprise, but I would tell you it is something we still grieve when they are missed, even today.

For Libby's first birthday, we blew it out. We probably invited between fifty and a hundred people, including several of Libby's doctors who had become friends with Mary and me. It was an incredible celebration for our whole family, including our extended family who had walked each step of our journey thus far, right by our side. And so, we were adjusting—getting used to our "new normal." Some of the fog of emotion was burning away. Not all of it, of course. There were certainly good days and bad days, good appointments and a lot of bad ones too, but we were moving forward.

Now, I don't know how she wouldn't have, but Libby fit into our family immediately and perfectly. Obviously, Mary and I were absolutely crazy about our little girl. Like each of our children, God had given us a unique and special love for her and there wasn't anything we wouldn't do to provide for and protect her. Our older children also loved having a baby sister. They doted on Libby and cared for her from the moment we brought her home until today. I think even though they were young, both of my children had an instinctive understanding that Libby was special and required more care than a typical baby brother or sister might have. One of the absolute blessings of God has been the way He has shaped my children's hearts by using their sisters' disabilities to widen their capacity for love. God has used Libby to mold the most incredible spirit of tenderness, compassion, and care in Kathryn, Coleman and Campbell, and that is truer today than ever before.

Libby fit with us, and our family also fit around Libby. While it took a little while for us to steady our legs beneath us again, once we adjusted to life with Libby, we went right back into the busy routine of a young family with three small children, very actively involved in our church and in the community where we lived. And once we began to catch our breath and move forward with our lives, adjusting to this "new normal" and the calm after our storm, God really began giving our family a passion for other families who were themselves experiencing their own seasons of suffering. Whether that suffering was a child facing an illness or an individual with special needs, Libby had become a front door that allowed us to meet so many other wonderful people. We began to learn so much about the often forgotten, marginalized, and least-known people in our society, the disability community.

In his book, *Walking with God through Pain and Suffering*, Pastor Tim Keller reminds his readers of how the Apostle Paul knew first hand through affliction and suffering that God was using those hardships to minister to others in suffering seasons of their own. Keller writes, "Paul's suffering drive him into God and his unfathomable comforts. We have been looking at many of those in this volume—deeper views of God's glory, and heart-changing appreciation of Christ's suffering, insights into life and human nature. What does Paul do with those insights? He shares them with others in affliction, who then through their sufferings find the deeper comforts too. The implication is that these sufferers in turn become comforters to others—and on and on it goes. The church becomes a community of profound consolation, a place where you get enormous support for suffering and where people find themselves growing, through their troubles, into the persons God wants them to become." [14]

As I continued to pursue my vocational calling into the ministry, God opened doors and made a way for me to transition out of the landscape business and into full-time ministry on staff at a large and very well-respected church in the Dallas area. I learned so much so quickly from observing other ministers on our staff and discovering how a healthy church should work. I also continued my educational pursuits, attending seminary part-time and online. I was growing and learning ministry both through hands-on, practical experiences in our church where I worked, as well as in my studies and from my professors who helped me to discover the biblical and academic underpinnings for what I was called to do. But in all, it was Libby who best prepared me for the special responsibility of pastoral care.

Pastors and authors John Piper and Justin Taylor talk about the ministry of comfort in their book, *Suffering and the Sovereignty of God*, when they write, "But when you've passed through your own fiery trials, and found God to be true to what he says, you have real help to offer. You have firsthand experience of both his sustaining grace and his purposeful design. He has kept you through pain; he reshaped you more into his image. You've found that what this entire hymn says is *true*. What you are experiencing from God, you can give away in increasing measure to others. You are learning both the tenderness and the clarity necessary to help sanctify another person's deepest distress. 2 Corinthians 1:4 says it best: "[God] comforts us in all our affliction so that we will be able to comfort those who are in any affliction with the comfort with which we ourselves are comforted by God." That word "comfort" (or "encourage" in other translations) does not simply mean solace or inspiration. It means God's transformative compassion, the perfect union of kindness and candor. He speaks the truth in love so that we grow up to do the same. Notice how wise love is a "generalizable skill." What you learn from God in your *particular* affliction becomes helpful to others in *any* affliction." [15]

Libby taught me about the anxiousness that accompanies the surgical waiting room. Libby taught me what a family wants to hear from a visitor and what they do not. Libby taught me what words comfort a family in a moment of prayer and what words do not. Libby taught me about the disappointment of unfavorable test results and the letdown of a doctor's diagnosis. God used Libby to educate me in the privilege of pastoral ministry unlike any team member on our staff or any professor of my class.

And Mary was experiencing the same growth opportunities too. Time after time friends would share the name and contact information of someone who had just received a difficult diagnosis for their child. Mary was asked over and over again if she would reach out and encourage that mother and pray with them. Sometimes, Mary would be able to share learning experiences or a doctor's information, but other times she just listened to a devastated mom weep over her child, knowing Mary was a safe person for that to take place. I have watched with great joy as I have seen God use my bride countless times to minister to other parents and families who find themselves navigating similar waters to ours. Mary has a unique gift that the Lord has cultivated in her to exhibit unbelievable compassion and care for others who are suffering while knowing intuitively the best ways to serve those families practically as they move ahead in their own journeys and struggles. We were learning, and God was using Libby as His instructor for the teaching that, while things might be calm after our storm, there is always someone else in the middle of their own storm and we have been given a unique privilege to help them if we can.

Randy Alcorn explains the ministry of comfort that Mary and I have been given this way, "The comfort God gives us in our suffering prepares us to comfort others who suffer as we have. One of God's purposes in our suffering is to prepare us to serve others, especially those who suffer as we have—for instance, from an addiction, miscarriage, abortion, infertility, divorce, or the loss of a spouse or child. Paul says, 'The God of all comfort … comforts us in all our troubles, so that we can comfort those in any trouble with the comfort we ourselves have received from God' (2 Corinthians 1:3–4). The common ground of suffering breaks down barriers of wealth, education, vocation and age. People in hospital waiting rooms often take an interest in one another's suffering and loved ones. They sail together on the same ship, riding the same rough waters." [16]

And in this, Mary and I have the most incredible opportunities to speak of God's goodness and to boast in God's grace because of the suffering that our Libby has endured. I tell people all the time that, while I might be a pastor, Libby is the greatest evangelist in the Bales family. She shares the Gospel more eloquently without being able to speak a word than I ever could in a thousand sermons I might preach.

This is the redemptive aim of God in working through bad to bring such good. This is what authors Larry Waters and Roy Zuck explain when they write, "Besides displaying one man's faith in God in times of suffering, the book of Job also has a 'missionary' purpose. That is, a believer's suffering should be viewed, as seen in Job's experience, as an opportunity to witness not only to God's sovereignty but also to His goodness, justice, grace, and love to the nonbelieving world. Often the purpose of the Book of Job is seen simply as concerned with the sovereignty of God and man's response to His will. But the book is also part of the progressive revelation of God's purpose and mission, so that the book is, in a sense, missional and evangelistic. That is, as believers undergo undeserved suffering, they are witnesses to nonbelievers of God's goodness, justice, grace, and love. ... Job is one of the first illustrations of an individual whom God used to demonstrate that mission involves God's redemptive purposes." [17] God was at work in our family, through our story. It was painful to be sure, but there was no denying His goodness toward us throughout. Things had calmed down. The storm had passed and we were enjoying the calmer weather. We tried to help anyone we could navigate their storms, as we were able to share what we had seen and learned through our own.

And so between the therapies, doctors' appointments, my work, the older kids' school and schedules, and all that was the rhythm of our regular life, things began to settle down in our world and we resumed a very "new normal" life for our family. Mary and I began praying about growing our family, and once we had a peace about it we decided we would try for a baby again. After the disappointment of another miscarriage, we were blessed to find out that Mary was expecting again, another little girl, and she was due sometime in the middle of November of 2011. Things were calm again, but *this time* it was *before* the storm and not after.

Chapter 7

"COUNTED WORTHY"

It's been my experience that much of life can be summarized in the memories being made while we're living it. This reality is because our memories are tied to our moments of significance. Most of the time, the more important the event, the more powerful and vivid the memory will be that is associated with it. For example, when I was growing up, I remember my first home run in little league baseball. I've got great memories that are tied to that. I can remember the first time I went hunting with my dad. I've got wonderful memories which are also tied to that. I remember as a child when our home burned down. I have vivid and sad memories directly linked with that. I can remember some very competitive sporting events around the house with my two brothers. I have some very funny memories that are tied to that as well. I remember my first date with Mary. I have some of my most tender memories in close connection with that.

That is how memories work. They are images in our mind which trigger the recollection of significant moments and events from our life. The events surrounding the birth of our fourth child, our daughter Hannah, have probably given me the single most vivid memory I have in my life. Certainly, the events around my salvation, my marriage, the birth of my children, and my calling into the ministry are also very special and each very unique. But, with Hannah, I experienced what has been the most powerfully surreal moment I have ever known, and it has forever changed my life. Let me explain...

Mary's pregnancy with Hannah was completely normal. Like all of her pregnancies before, Mary hadn't experienced any unusual symptoms and there were no serious problematic findings during any of her doctor's appointments at all. Yet, because of the severity of Libby's genetic condition and in an abundance of prudence and caution, Mary's doctor insisted that we see a prenatal specialist in coordination with his ongoing care throughout the pregnancy. This process included some genetic counseling from a genetics specialist in the doctor's office. She made sure we were made very aware of all of our options for genetic testing in utero and then, depending on those findings, all of the options for response, most especially the option for termination if desired. As is no surprise to anyone, termination would never be an option for our family to consider. Our biblical convictions have taught us that all life is a gift from God and that every person has been created in the image of God. The Bible clearly teaches that humanity is distinct from the rest of creation in this truth. *"Then God said, 'Let us make man in our image, after our likeness. And let them have dominion over the fish of the sea and over the birds of the heavens and over the livestock and over all the earth and over every creeping thing that creeps on the earth.'"* (Genesis 1:26 ESV). Therefore, because humanity bears God's image and has been made in His likeness, all human life has an intrinsic value, dignity, and worth, none of which is contingent upon ability, gifting, or health.

I appreciate how mother and author Stephanie Hubach elaborates on the understanding of the imago Dei, when she writes, "When the image of God within is central to our understanding of humanity, it sends a powerful message about human value to the world around us. Our culture often measures personal value as a function of productivity. The degree to which we are able to contribute to society is the degree to which we are valued. In God's economy, however, human value is defined by the Creator Himself through the imprint of His image in mankind. Others take notice, not merely when we say this is true, but when we live like it is true. Our actions ought to declare, 'You are incredibly valuable!' to everyone we meet. In the same way, the *powerful message* of the gospel is demonstrated when we respond to others in grace-based actions. Our competitive culture is uncomfortable with the concept of weakness. When people see us acknowledge our frailties and intentionally engage others in the areas of their brokenness, we live out the gospel of grace in powerful ways." [18]

When we were getting down to the finish line in Mary's pregnancy with Hannah, because Libby had come early, we were a little better prepared this time, in case Hannah decided to do the same. But, in God's perfect timing, at almost thirty-eight weeks, on October 31, 2011, at 1:25 p.m., Hannah Jane Bales was born weighing five pounds twelve ounces. Unlike any of our deliveries before, but because of our family's new medical history with Libby, we had a host of people in the room for Hannah's arrival. There were extra doctors and nurses and it proved to be a good thing too, as Hannah, like Libby before her, needed some extra support to regulate her breathing and was taken relatively soon after delivery to the NICU for close monitoring and care.

Despite the ease of Mary's delivery (said most cautiously as the guy who has never delivered a baby before) and in the absence of any complications associated with Hannah's birth, our little girl still needed some extra time to develop and receive that added support that an excellent NICU can provide. Hannah went through a fairly extensive litany of tests and close observation while staying at the hospital. The added attention she received was in part because her lungs needed strengthening and she needed to learn how to feed without stressing her body out by not breathing efficiently while she did it. Additionally, and probably more importantly, Hannah received extra attention and focus because of Libby's medical history and the similar ways the two girls presented at birth. Unlike Libby however, Hannah did not have any cardiovascular defects and she didn't have any malformations of her hands or feet. She did, however, have a polycystic left kidney, which was detected without major concern in utero, and she was also pretty small for being almost full-term at her delivery. All in all, Hannah was a seemingly much, much healthier baby than her older sister Libby. No heart defect. No malformation of her feet. It seems like we should have been relieved.

But … Mary and I never had a peace about her health. We wanted to, desperately. We tried and tried to convince ourselves that because she didn't have the same obvious medical problems as Libby, she certainly wouldn't carry a similar diagnosis. Unfortunately, we just couldn't shake the suspicion we had despite all of that. Our pediatrician and the hospital neonatologist both agreed that we had all of the cause and justification we would ever need to have Hannah's labs taken and for genetic testing to be done on her so we would know one way or the other. So we did. While staying at the hospital and recovering in the NICU, Hannah's blood work was drawn and submitted to the laboratory for the necessary genetic mapping to be done so we might know if there was anything abnormal there or not.

After only seven days in the NICU, with Mary and I adopting the same routine of visitation as we had used with Libby, we were finally able to bring our little girl home. We were thrilled to be settling back into our routine. Libby was in full swing with her therapies and both Kathryn and Coleman were rocking along in school and extra-curricular activities, and our family moved quickly through the holidays and toward Christmas, adjusting to our "new normal" yet again. This time we were a family of six, with a newborn baby right in the thick of it. Mary and I were doing well. Kathryn, Coleman, and Libby were doing well. Hannah was doing well, although Mary and I had never escaped that suspicious feeling about her long-term health and we remained anxiously curious about the findings from the lab.

December 2, 2011, began as a very typical Friday for our family. Fridays are usually the day of the week when I'm out of the office and able to be most available to Mary and our kids for family time. And this particular Friday fit right into that mold. Mary and I had planned that evening to drop by and spend time with several of our small groups from church who were hosting Christmas parties which we had been invited to attend. It was scheduled to be a Friday like every other, which it was … until the phone rang. Mary came in with a concerned look on her face and told me that the pediatrician had called. She said the doctor told her that Hannah's lab results were in and he asked if we could stop by his office that day to discuss the findings together. We knew. Without hearing a word definitively, we both knew. We called my mom and made arrangements for her to come over to the house to watch the other kids at our home while we went to the doctor's office that afternoon for this appointment.

I know I mentioned before how great our pediatricians were, walking our family through these difficult moments with our girls, but truly, this incredibly kind couple applied their knowledge of medicine with their compassion for others and allowed us to enjoy the greatest confidence in their care. Despite the difficulty and tragedy of what we faced, they served as wonderful instruments of God's grace to us and I am forever grateful to them (and their staff) for the tenderness they showed us as we processed together so much related to the health of our family.

It felt like slow motion. If you have ever seen the Kevin Costner baseball movie, *For the Love of the Game*, then perhaps you will remember a phrase he coined, as the main character, while acting the role of a major league baseball pitcher playing in the game of his life. "Clear the mechanism." That was it. With just that simple phrase Costner's character could drown out all of the surrounding sights and sounds of a major league baseball stadium and could concentrate perfectly and intently on just himself, the batter, and his catcher. Everything got quiet. The game slowed way down. It felt as if the entire world was in slow motion. That is just about the only way I know to describe the feeling I had when our pediatrician told us that the lab results revealed Hannah had the exact same chromosomal abnormality as her sister Libby. Hannah was diagnosed with Trisomy 16p.

I'll never forget that moment. Our doctor was fighting back tears as he confirmed what Mary and I wanted to make absolutely sure we had heard correctly. "Trisomy 16p? Are you sure? I thought our geneticist said this was a mathematical impossibility and there was no one else like Libby that we could find? How? Is there a chance the test is wrong? But Hannah doesn't have the heart defect and her feet are just fine? This can't be right." Even though Mary and I had a suspicion that something might be wrong with Hannah, I was rapid-firing questions at our doctor, needing clarity as to how it could be this.

Mary and I sobbed. Our doctor cried with us. "I'm so sorry guys. I'm just so sorry." That's all he could muster as he watched our hearts break right in front of him. We were wrecked. I couldn't catch my breath. His little office began closing in on us, I couldn't reconcile what it was we were hearing. "Here we go again. God, I can't do this again." These were the thoughts that immediately flooded my mind. We were undone. Devastated. Destroyed. All over again.

Our doctor told us that he too was shocked for all of the scientific and mathematical reasons we had already asked about. He went on to say that he would have thought the lab confused Hannah's results for Libby's if the director of the laboratory himself had not called him personally to confirm that after repeating the test twice, the results were accurate. On paper, Hannah is a genetic twin of her sister Libby. I don't know the odds of this, and frankly, I don't care, but as you might have guessed by now, we are in rare air with our girls. And if I'm being honest with you, in that doctor's office that day, in that moment with that diagnosis read, it felt hard to breathe up there.

It took more than a few minutes for us to gather our composure. Everything had gone from the slow motion of the doctor sharing the test results to the speed of light as my mind began to race to all of the unknowns that come with Trisomy 16p. Our doctor kindly gave us all the time we needed to collect ourselves and so Mary and I waited until we were composed enough to walk out of his office without scaring all of the other children and families who were there to be seen. We hugged the doctors as we left, crying all over again on their shoulders, and we made our way slowly to my car.

Listen, I believe in the supernatural. I do, completely. But I will also admit that I think some of what people attribute to the supernatural is not, and if that makes me a skeptic, then so be it. Nevertheless, I believe in the supernatural. And what happened when Mary and I got into our car that day, I can only attribute to the supernatural work of God. When we got into the car, before we turned the ignition to start it up, I looked over at Mary and grabbed her hand. There was nothing supernatural about that, but there was something absolutely supernatural about what happened next. In my spirit, I felt God the Holy Spirit speak to me these words, "I have counted you worthy to get to do this twice." As clearly as I am writing this now or speaking it out loud to you in person, God spoke into my spirit that phrase exactly. We had been counted worthy. I looked over at Mary and through even more tears I shared what I felt God had just told me and she completely agreed, she felt it too. We were counted worthy by the God of the universe to care for, shepherd, protect, steward, provide for, teach, learn from, and love these two precious and rare gifts from God Himself. And what's more, because we have been entrusted with both Libby *and* Hannah, then God has counted us worthy to get to share in this joy *twice*!

Author Elisabeth Elliot rightly describes suffering as a gift, when she says, "But when we're talking about the gifts of God, we're talking about gifts that come from One who knows exactly what we need even though it is not necessarily to our tastes and preferences. And He gives us everything that is appropriate to the job that He wants us to do. And so, understanding that, we can say, yes, Lord, I'll take it. It would not have been my choice but knowing You love me, I will receive it and I understand that someday I'm going to understand the necessity for this thing. So I accept it. And then I can even go the step beyond and say thank You. Thank you, Lord." [19]

Friends, I tell you about our miracle moment not so that you might see our story and celebrate us, but so that you might see our story and celebrate *God*. My whole perspective changed in an instant, and not in any way because my circumstances did. No, I still had two daughters with very severe special needs and a massive

amount of medical complications and a very bleak
prognosis for their lives. My perspective changed because
my privilege was found. And please hear me, I don't mean
to trivialize the difficulty of our journey, it is hard, and I'll
share more about that in the chapters ahead, but it is also
rewarding and truly a privilege that God would entrust
the care of these rare gifts to us. This phrase, "counted
worthy," changes everything. God's glory being seen in our
story. In our suffering.

I wonder about how God's glory is being displayed
in your suffering. Have you thought about that? You
too have been counted worthy to endure something,
and God is using it to build something in you and
show something great about Himself through you.
Think about these words from authors D.A. Carson
and Kathleen Nielson, in their book, *Resurrection Life in
a World of Suffering.* "Let's say it right out and wonder
at it: suffering is actually part of God's plan (and so
necessary) to bring about the shining riches of praise and
glory and honor. Glory is shining forth of God's very
being. His glory is what He's after, shining forth even in
us! Gold can't begin to picture it. Of course we cannot
understand this glory without beginning at the cross,
with the suffering of our Savior on our behalf. There was
glory revealed. As we trust our Savior and then follow
after Him, what the apostle Paul says is true: our present
sufferings are not worth comparing with the glory that
is to be revealed in us (Rom. 8:18)—an eternal weight of
glory (2 Cor. 4:17)." [20]

How about you? Have you ever stopped to wonder if
your suffering, as difficult and painful as it might be,

isn't something you might have been entrusted with for a purpose greater than you could ever know without it? What have you been counted worthy to endure? Who have you been counted worthy to love? How have you been counted worthy of your suffering? Perspective changes when privilege is found. It is a privilege that God has counted us worthy to be the parents of each one of our children and, in particular, Libby and Hannah. Have you discovered your privilege so that it might change your perspective?

Chapter 8

"CLARITY"

A few years ago, almost in perfect coordination with my turning forty, my eyesight began to diminish. It felt like this happened overnight, but I have needed the help of reading glasses ever since. I think I first noticed this when I was reading a menu, but I chalked it up to bad lighting in the restaurant. It got worse. I was having the hardest time seeing the words clearly enough to read anything as quickly as I wanted, unless, on those rare occasions, I discovered that perfect distance to hold the paper or book away from my face, so everything came into focus. After struggling for a while, both with my eyesight and perhaps even more with my vanity, with Mary's encouragement, I finally went and got fitted for glasses. Wow! What an unbelievable difference. It shouldn't have surprised me knowing how difficult seeing my Bible or a restaurant menu or my kids' homework had become, but it did. I was shocked. The clarity of sight because of the addition and benefit of my glasses changed everything. Clarity always does.

In a very similar way, this is how I felt when God granted me the clarity of calling in the parking lot of our pediatrician's office that December day in 2011. On the heels of a devastating diagnosis, and what I thought would be a downward spiral for the second time, I discovered that God had already begun to work out the most clarifying reality for me and that He was using the journey with Libby and Hannah to do it.

Just as before when we began to adjust to our "new normal" with Libby, we finally embraced the challenges of this life and we jumped headfirst into the ministry aspects that come with having a family member or friend with a chronic illness or some type of special need. God began growing us through both His Word and our own personal experiences in a deeper understanding of how His sovereignty and goodness worked, most especially in the midst of unexplained suffering and tragedy.

One morning in my personal devotion, I found myself reading that familiar passage I referenced earlier from John Chapter 9. Only this time it was different. Rather than simply staying confused as I had been before, God gave me some of the greatest clarity in my life as the powerful words of Christ leapt off the pages of Scripture and into my heart that day. *"As he passed by, he saw a man blind from birth. And his disciples asked him, 'Rabbi, who sinned, this man or his parents, that he was born blind?' Jesus answered, 'It was not that this man sinned, or his parents, but that the works of God might be displayed in him. We must work the works of him who sent me while it is day; night is coming, when no one can work. As long as I am in the world, I am the light of the world.'"* (John 9:1–5 ESV).

Do you remember the dilemma that the disciples and I had? In the same way that I had struggled in the fog of confusion about Libby's suffering, the disciples were looking for a reason why this man was born blind. The disciples sought an explanation as to what unmerited human suffering could be attributed to at its origin. And in some ways, so did I. However, on this particular morning, what jumped out at me from off these pages of Scripture was clear. In His reply, Jesus meets the question of His disciples' head-on. This is just another of the characteristics that I'm so grateful for in our Savior. He is unafraid of and unapologetic about the truth. His answer is tremendously controversial but completely thorough and altogether helpful. Jesus's response is that not only is this man's disability not some consequence of personal sin, but it was, additionally, not any consequence of that man's parents' sin either. Jesus sought to dismiss not only their own narrow view but also any potential extended application from their line of reasoning. Jesus thoughtfully and purposefully dismantles any bad ideas that surround the realities of our fallen and broken world. Jesus explains that God is not punitive in causing someone to suffer, but rather, is gracious in His working good amid the suffering.

Author Dave Furman summarizes the idea this way, when he writes, "Our frail bodies are not a mistake. Our frailty is not a surprise to God nor are we weak as a result of Him being powerless to give us stronger bodies. The fall brought disease and death, but through our weaknesses, God shows off His all-surpassing power—to us and to the world." [21]

"In His grace, Jesus emphasizes that the object deserving the most curiosity is not in fact the blind man, but God who works in him. Did you see it? Look again at verse three, *Jesus answered, "It was not that this man sinned, or his parents, but that the works of God might be displayed in him"'* (John 9:3 ESV). The reality of whatever suffering, circumstance, or difficulty a person faces, is never actually about that suffering, circumstance, or difficulty. It is always about our God who is actively at work in those things. Keller gives this brief summary of Christ's work here, when he says, 'In John 9, Jesus heals a blind man and takes pains to show His disciples that he was not in that condition because of his sin or that of his parents, but in order to fulfill God's inscrutable purposes.'" [22]

Likewise, Randy Alcorn gives an incredibly insightful and illustrative explanation of this New Testament story found in John 9, where he explains, "God can use suffering to display His work in you. When Christ's disciples asked whose sin lay behind a man born blind, Jesus said, 'Neither this man nor his parents sinned' (John 9:3). Jesus then redirected His disciples from thinking about the *cause* of the man's disability to consider the *purpose* for it. He said, 'This happened *so that* the work of God might be displayed in his life.' Eugen Peterson paraphrases Christ's words this way: 'You're asking the wrong question. You're looking for someone to blame. There is no such cause-effect here. Look instead for what God can do.'" (MSG).

"Nick Vujicic entered this world without arms or legs. Both his mom and his dad, an Australian pastor, felt devastated by their firstborn son's condition. 'If God is a God of love,' they said, 'then why would he let something like this happen, and especially to committed Christians?' But they chose to trust God despite their questions.

"Nick struggled at school where other students bullied and rejected him. 'At that stage in my childhood,' he said,

'I could understand His love to a point. But … I still got hung up on the fact that if God really loved me, why did He make me like this? I wondered if I'd done something wrong and began to feel certain that this must be true.'

"Thoughts of suicide plagued Nick until one day the fifteen-year-old read the story in John 9 about the man born blind: 'but that the works of God should be revealed in him' (NKJV). He surrendered his life to Christ. Now, at age twenty-six, he's earned a Bachelor's degree and encourages others as a motivational speaker. 'Due to the emotional struggles I had experienced with bullying, self-esteem, and loneliness,' Nick says, 'God began to instill a passion of sharing my story and experiences to help others cope with whatever challenge they might have in their lives. Turning my struggles into something that would glorify God and bless others, I realized my purpose! The Lord was going to use me to encourage and inspire others to live to their fullest potential and not let anything in the way of accomplishing their hopes and dreams. God's purposes became clearer to me and now I'm fully convinced and understand that His glory is revealed as He uses me just the way I am. And even more wonderful, He can use me in ways others can't be used.'" [23]

And for this dad, perhaps the single greatest reality for me of what Jesus said when He answered the disciples' question and spoke of the works of God in suffering, is that this declaration is given *prior* to the healing taking place. Did you hear that? God is at work, and His work is not contingent upon healing happening as we have asked or expected that it should. God is absolutely, completely, totally, and lovingly at work in Libby's and Hannah's lives, and that declaration is 100% true regardless of whether or not He heals them on this side of eternity or the other.

Do I still pray for healing? Yes, all the time. Almost every day. Sometimes the prayers are little. "God, would you please ease whatever is bothering the girls since they can't tell us what hurts? God, would you allow this meeting with the girl's teacher to be positive and encouraging as we gage the progress they've made?" Other times, it has been huge. "God, would you please stop the seizures. God, I'm begging you, would you clear out the pneumonia? God, would you realign their chromosomes in their sleep?" Yes, I've prayed *that* prayer many, many times. Why? Because He could. And sometimes God has answered the little ones, and sometimes He has not. And sometimes God has answered the big ones, and sometimes He has not. But His workmanship is evident in their suffering, in their trials, in our family's struggle, and it has never been contingent upon His healing for that to be true. I'll share more in the chapters ahead, but the works of God in the life of our family are so obvious and gracious and good. In fact, it's God's good work in our girls' lives that led me to write this book.

Again, I resonate with mother and author Stephanie Hubach's words when she says, "It's time to tell the truth about disability: it is a normal part of life in an abnormal world. We are all recipients of the blessedness of creation and the brokenness of the fall. Upholding a biblical perspective of disability really matters, because when we see our world truthfully, we can view ourselves more correctly. When we view ourselves more correctly, we can also regard others more accurately. And when we regard others more accurately, we are more likely to respond to them appropriately." [24] The value of my girls is intrinsic and given by God who made them. And this value and worth does not change based upon ability *or* disability. Therefore, while the suffering is tough, God's work in and through those challenging moments is just as tangible and powerful as any physical healing and restoration might also provide.

But, because physical healing isn't the only evidence of God's work, does this mean that God doesn't care about suffering? Absolutely not! The Bible tells us in the book of Hebrews that Jesus Himself is our empathetic High Priest, interceding on behalf of those whom He has saved (Hebrews 4:14-16). Paul Tripp explains God's understanding of suffering by saying, "Crying out to God in your moment of need is like talking to a dear friend whom you are comfortable talking to because you know that she knows exactly what you are going through. But there is more. God not only understands the broken space that is our current address; He inhabited that space in the person of His Son Jesus. This means that the One to whom you cry has firsthand knowledge of the things you're dealing with. It is frustrating to every sufferer to share their travail with people who don't have a clue and can't relate because they have no firsthand knowledge of what you're talking about. Jesus is not just a student of our suffering; He became a firsthand participant in it." [25]

Likewise, Dave Furman explains the empathy of God in his book, *Kiss the Wave*, when he writes, "Jesus faced all the pain and disappointment of life as a human being. He knows how it feels to be tempted and to suffer loss. Jesus knows what it is like to cry tears, to feel betrayed. He was rejected by those close to Him, and He felt physical affliction. He was ignored by His friends, and He tasted death. Jesus identifies with us in every way. He faced torment at the greatest level when He was forsaken by God the Father at the cross, crushed by the wrath of God and the weight of our sins. Even in our worst trials, when the waves are crashing upon us, we can say in faith: 'Jesus you understand. You understand what I am going through.' And He does. He understands what it's like to be a teenager. He understands what it's like to have shooting nerve pain in His body. He knows what it's like to be poor, to be mocked, beaten, and abused. He knows what it's like to be betrayed by a friend. He knows what it's like to face trials as an innocent one. He knows. He understands our pain. How comforting that He 'gets' us." [26]

Suffering can look so many different ways and take so many different forms, and God cares about all of it. Have you been betrayed? So has Jesus. Have you been persecuted? So has Jesus. Have you lost loved ones? So has Jesus. Have you suffered physically? So has Jesus. He knows. He gets it, and He cares deeply for us and for our suffering.

Fellow sufferer and personal hero to me and my family, Joni Eareckson Tada talks about God's understanding of suffering, along with her co-author Steven Estes in their book, *When God Weeps,* in this way, "This is good news for the suffering soul. The Son of God did not exempt Himself from affliction but lived through it and learned from it. Once that process was complete, He became the source of help for all who obey Him. Should we suffer? 'A student is not above his teacher, nor a servant above his master,' says the One who learned obedience from what he suffered.

'It is enough for the student to be like his teacher, and the servant like his master' (Matthew 10:24–25). We open our Bibles and find that God has His reasons for allowing suffering, not just in the larger realm, but in the life of the individual. Learning some of those reasons can make all the difference in the world." [27]

Remember the words of Jesus from His famous Sermon on the Mount, *"Therefore I tell you, do not be anxious about your life, what you will eat or what you will drink, nor about your body, what you will put on. Is not life more than food, and the body more than clothing? Look at the birds of the air: they neither sow nor reap nor gather into barns, and yet your heavenly Father feeds them. Are you not of more value than they? And which of you by being anxious can add a single hour to his span of life? And why are you anxious about clothing? Consider the lilies of the field, how they grow: they neither toil nor spin, yet I tell you, even Solomon in all his glory was not arrayed like one of these. But if God so clothes the grass of the field, which today is alive and tomorrow is thrown into the oven, will he not much more clothe you, O you of little faith?"* (Matthew 6:25–30 ESV). We're not birds! We're not wildflowers! We are God's image-bearers in creation! We've been imprinted with God's image and likeness. We are infinitely valuable to God. God knows about our suffering and God deeply cares about us in our suffering. My daughters have NEVER faced a surgery, or hospital stay, or doctor's appointment, or therapy that God wasn't keenly aware of, completely involved in, and deeply concerned for … NEVER! That is clear. That clarity gives comfort. Joni Eareckson Tada reminds us of this work of God in her book, *A Place of Healing*, where she says, "While I'm not saying God enjoys watching us struggle, His Word clearly indicates He allows wounds to prick and pierce us. But that doesn't mean He has stopped caring. God expresses His care in different ways. As many have said so eloquently, sometimes He delivers us *from* the storm and at other times He delivers us *through* the storm." 28

Finally, in expounding on this truth, Jesus goes further with His thought by saying, *"We must work the works of him who sent me while it is day; night is coming, when no one can work"* (John 9:4 ESV). It might be this verse that can be the most misunderstood of the first four from this chapter. Jesus appears to be explaining to His disciples that all things, even suffering, should be seen in light of God's ability to work through them, as long as one is alive. Jesus adds a temporal component to the question. In addition to the question held as to the cause of the blind man's condition, Jesus elects to address an apparent eschatological truth in His response to His disciples at the same time. Jesus places an emphasis on God's glory being made known *now*, referencing the idea that at some time in the future there will be no more work done. God's glory will continue to be known, but it won't involve any suffering for it to be seen. There will be no more work in suffering because there will be no more suffering! This is such good news.

I love how this is described in some of the incredible books on suffering I have read over these last several years. Authors Piper and Taylor express this incredible hope by saying, "When we are in the pit of despair we must look around and see that only God can bring us out. There is no other hope. And what's more is that God himself is committed to bringing us out. He alone is holy and therefore he alone can help us. Yes, the night is long and the weeping intense, but the morning is coming. And as we wait for the coming dawn, the return of the Son of God, we can know that we are not alone. While we are on earth, there often will be deliverance from many of our sufferings—there will be many mornings that will dawn and bring with them joy. But the ultimate morning comes when Jesus returns. That is when the true shout for joy will come and when all tears will be wiped away (Rev. 21:4)." [29]

Likewise, when speaking of this hope working in concert with our sorrow, author Mark Vroegop shares this thought, "Finally, we've seen that Christians lament expectantly. Knowing God's goodness and believing in his sovereignty cause us to pray for divine intervention to the painful paradoxes of life. We know the brokenness of sin that causes all lament. And we believe the death and resurrection of Jesus inaugurated the defeat of sin, death, and all tears. In our sorrow, we long for the day when lament will be no more: 'He will wipe away every tear from their eyes, and death shall be no more, neither shall there be mourning, nor crying, nor pain anymore, for the former things have passed away' (Rev. 21:4).

"One of the greatest joys of the new heavens and the new earth will be the absence of all songs of sorrow. Perhaps we'll sing the Psalms, but we'll not sing all of them. In God's presence there will be no need to lament. All our complaints will be complete. Our requests will have been answered. Praise will be the air we breathe. Heavenly praise will replace our earthly groaning." [30]

I'm crying as I write this now, overwhelmed by the thought that there is a day coming when my girls will be whole. When they will never endure another test, never suffer more pneumonia, never convulse from another seizure. Libby and Hannah will walk with us, talk to us, and run to Jesus! The Apostle John visualized that day as recorded in the book of Revelation. *"Then I saw a new heaven and a new earth, for the first heaven and the first earth had passed away, and the sea was no more. And I saw the holy city, New Jerusalem, coming down out of heaven from God, prepared as a bride adorned for her husband. And I heard a loud voice from the throne saying, 'Behold, the dwelling place of God is with man. He will dwell with them, and they will be his people, and God himself will be with them as their God. He will wipe away every tear from their eyes, and death shall be no more, neither shall there be mourning, nor crying, nor pain anymore, for the former things have passed away.'"* (Revelation 21:1–4 ESV). That day is coming, and we (I) trust in God for each day between this one and that one. That's how we (I) endure suffering. Trusting in God who is working in it and believing in God for the day it will be no more.

Again, I find strength in the words of other authors who have shared their hopes for that glorious day to come. Tim Keller says, "The resurrection of the body means that we do not merely receive a consolation for the life we have lost but a restoration of it. We not only get the bodies and lives we had but the bodies and lives we wished for but never before received. We get a glorious, perfect, unimaginably rich life in a renewed material world." [31] And Dave Furman envisions this biblical hope, that the resurrection of Jesus has made our reality, by saying, "The truth of the resurrection gives us real hope. If you can't kneel and you can't dance and you can't run, in the resurrection you will dance perfectly. If you are lonely, in the resurrection you will have perfect love. If your heart is empty, in the resurrection you will be thoroughly filled. If you are depressed, in the resurrection your joy will be complete. Christian, if you are facing grave illness or even death, the resurrection gives you hope that in the moment you die, you will be with Christ." [32]

Finally, when Jesus answers the disciples' question, He also offers a shift in the focus in verse four. Jesus shows us that God is clearly the subject, not the sufferer nor the suffering. God, as *"him who sent me"*, is clearly seen as the one to whom deference and glory belong. The writer even uses grammatical tenses to address a present problem from a future perspective. God is the hero in every story of suffering because He is the one working good in the midst of it. We might not always see it or be aware of Him while He is doing it, but the fact that it is being done is always true. Author Elisabeth Elliot gets to the point quickly when she says, "And I've come to see that it's through the deepest suffering that God has taught me the deepest lessons. And if we'll trust Him for it, we can come through to the unshakable assurance that He's in charge. He has a loving purpose. And He can transform something terrible into something wonderful. Suffering is never for nothing." [33]

This idea of God at work in difficulty is one that is woven throughout the Scriptures. Most of us have heard some of these verses quoted at one time or another. Sometimes, they've even been shared out of context and in a way that was intended to help but ended up hurting instead (I'll talk more about that hurt in the next chapter.). Perhaps someone has shared Romans 8:28 with you, in the middle of your suffering. *"And we know that for those who love*

God all things work together for good, for those who are called according to his purpose." Have you ever heard that verse and wondered, "Good? How is what I'm suffering good? How is what Libby and Hannah are dealing with good?" I know I have. But be reminded, if it's in God's Word then it is true, and it can be trusted. And God's Word says *all things*. Not *some* things. Not *most* things. All things!

Paul David Tripp gives help in understanding the goodness of God and the suffering of man when he writes, "When people lift Romans 8:28 out of its immediate context they understand it to mean what it does not mean. The way to understand any single Bible passage is to remember that Scripture interprets Scripture. The key to understanding the true hope of this passage is to understand the 'good' that Paul is writing about. Verses 29 and 30 tell us. The 'good' that is guaranteed in this passage is our redemption. Even before he made the world, God made the decision that his work in us would be completed no matter what. This means that the grace you and I reach out for in our times of trouble is never shaky or at risk; it is a present expression of a plan that was settled before this world began. It is so good to know that when things in you and around you have been damaged or compromised, nothing can damage, interrupt, or stop your true security, which is found in God and his grace poured out for you. This proper understanding of this wonderful passage gives hope even when you look around and have no hope." [34]

So then, how can all things be working together for good, unless God is involved in them? Here's what I mean. Our world is completely broken, we've covered that. Sin has wrecked what God had made perfect. The consequences of this brokenness where we find ourselves are that without help or intervention, not *all* things can be working together for good because not *everything* is, in fact, good. But God, by the very definition of His character, is completely and only good. So, if God is *not* at work, then all things cannot be working together for good. However, because God *is* at work, then things can work for good, because God Himself is good. Good doesn't happen apart from God. This is a reality and certainly one which would include suffering. Again, going back to the point I made earlier, I believe this is why Jesus said that God's workmanship could be declared in the blind man's life, prior to his physical healing happening yet. Of course, we know that by the time you get down to verses six and seven of John Chapter 9, the blind man does have his sight physically, miraculously restored, but the declaration of God's workmanship came first.

David Powlison speaks of God's working good in the midst of bad by saying, "Affliction itself is not good, but God works what is very good, bringing the ignorant and wayward back home. Faith's enduring and alert dependency on the Lord is one of the Spirit's finest fruits. And you bear that fruit only when you have lived through something hard." [35]

Still further, the apostle Paul says: *"And I am sure of this, that he who began a good work in you will bring it to completion at the day of Jesus Christ"* (Philippians 1:6 ESV). God begins and finishes His good work. All of His work. Even the good work He does through suffering. Likewise, this truth is echoed even in the Old Testament Scriptures as God promises His covenant people of His intention to work on and in their lives. *"For I know the plans I have for you, declares the Lord, plans for welfare and not for evil, to give you a future and a hope"* (Jeremiah 29:11 ESV). God has good plans for His people, and that would certainly have included those plans which involved seasons of suffering for Israel.

Anyone, who has ever tried to explain away God as being an uninvolved, uncaring, unapproachable being, absolutely does not know Him. But what Jesus wants to communicate to His disciples in John Chapter 9, and I believe, on that particular morning, He wanted to communicate to me as well, is that in the midst of this broken reality that is our suffering, our focus should not be on the suffering itself but rather on our God who is at work, doing good, in the middle of the suffering. I gained some much-needed clarity that day. My personal understanding of the goodness of God in the midst of suffering has grown. I believe as finite beings, we hold in tension the difficulty of human suffering and the reality of the sovereignty of God. This truth, while difficult for us to fully comprehend, is what makes our faith so necessary. It is in fact suffering, which has grown my faith. It is still growing, and I am still learning. In her book, *Through Gates of Splendor*, author Elisabeth Elliot says, "God is the God of human history, and He is at work continuously, mysteriously, accomplishing His eternal purposes in us, through us, for us, and in spite of us." [36]

Admittedly, this hasn't always been an enjoyable lesson to learn and it has certainly come with more than a few broken-hearted, angry, and confused questions being hurled at God along the way. But I am learning. I'm seeing more clearly, and clarity that comes from God is always a good thing. Here is what I believe we must learn to rightly embrace a healthy theology of suffering: The works of God are not limited to or contingent upon the physical healing of God! **Ours is not a God *for* the trials or a God *from* the trials. No, ours is a God *in* the trials, working for our good and His glory whether we recognize it or not.**

Chapter 9

"CRUEL"

I'm writing this chapter today during the week between Christmas and the new year. We have just finished a very busy season of ministry at our church, culminated by an incredible day of Christmas Eve worship services. I'm exhausted, but for all of the best reasons. Admittedly, however, in the busyness of the last several weeks, I didn't get to enjoy the traditional practice of watching as many Christmas movies as I normally do. Our family did enjoy one movie night a few weeks ago by watching *Elf*, starring Will Ferrell, and I think the movie *Home Alone* was on in the background quite a bit in the last couple of weeks as well, but some of the other staples just got missed this year.

One Christmas movie tradition that I know a lot of people practice is watching all of the Hallmark holiday movies. As I understand it, these movies begin gearing up on a regular rotation for about the last six weeks leading up to Christmas. I confess that I've never had any desire to sit down and watch a Hallmark movie. I have nothing against anyone else who does that or against Hallmark in general, but each one of their movies seem to have the same basic formula with only variables in character and story. They all seem to similarly wind down with a very happy ending.

Or, at least, that's the gist of the formula as I've been told and seen mocked online.

Maybe people have a growing fascination with these films because everyone knows that life isn't really like a Hallmark movie. Not everything has a picturesque happy ending where the characters are all smiling as the credits begin to roll. Life is hard. Life is messy. Sometimes, life can be flat-out cruel. And it doesn't take anyone long to learn that our difficult, messy, and sometimes cruel life includes suffering. In fact, because sin is common to everyone, then likewise suffering is common to everyone as well. Author Elisabeth Elliot defines suffering this way, "Suffering is having what you don't want or wanting what you don't have." [37] And what's fascinating is that there is a limitless number of things that cause us as people to be different, but very few things that we all have in common.

For example, I live in a suburb just north of Dallas, Texas. The professional football team we cheer for is the Dallas Cowboys. We love our Cowboys. We're committed to our Cowboys and yet, in a city of our size, you might be surprised at just how many people are fans of teams other than the Dallas Cowboys. Perhaps because they have moved to Texas from other parts of the country or maybe because technology allows a person to watch and support any team at any time from anywhere. Whatever the reason, there is never a shortage of people who will debate you on which team is better, yours or theirs (admittedly, a sad debate for us Cowboys fans to have in recent years). But regardless of what team you cheer for, and how much a person does not have in common with that rival fan, the one certain commonality shared among everyone everywhere is that we are all sinners and everyone either has already or will at some point, experience suffering in their life. Sin and its consequences of suffering are universal. No one escapes it.

In the book, *Joy in the Sorrow,* author Matt Chandler describes the cruel commonality of suffering by saying, "Suffering is the common denominator of all humanity in this world, isn't it? All of us are marked by scars of some sort, though not all are ones you can see. Waiting rooms and hospitals and gravesites don't play favorites. Rich and poor. Old and young. Every ethnicity and every generation. All under the same curse of a broken and bruised world where things don't work the way they were supposed to. Suffering is a part of every human experience." [38]

In pastoral ministry, the questions, or a version of them, which I am asked most often are, "Why do bad things happen to good people?" or "If God is good, why is there bad and evil in the world at all?" These are great questions. I will make my best attempt to answer them in this chapter but understand that the burden beneath each one is rooted in the pain common to all. That pain is suffering. Our family has endured a great deal of suffering.

Between Libby and Hannah, we have made more emergency room visits than I can count. Our girls have had dozens of hospitalizations, totaling months and months of time admitted and receiving treatment and care. I think Libby has had nine surgical procedures requiring full anesthesia and Hannah has had three. Libby has been admitted to the Pediatric ICU (PICU) three times with infections or pneumonia and Hannah has spent more than six weeks in the PICU in the last two years alone. When we lived in East Texas, we were transported by medical ambulance to a children's hospital in Dallas seven times and flown by air ambulance twice.

We've lived the ups and downs of trauma too. This includes the most terrifying moment of my life when Hannah crashed from a severe bout with pneumonia in 2018, which I already detailed in the first chapter of this book. I've already said how hard it is for me to describe the personal agony I felt, standing at the foot of her bed in the emergency room and watching the doctor and nurses bag and revive Hannah just long enough for a tube to be inserted down her throat and a respirator to be turned on. I'll never forget that moment. I'll never get over the sensory overload which can accompany such a traumatic event. The sight of people in and out of the room, working furiously trying to save your child. The sound of machines beeping and people barking orders and my own heart beating out loud. The sterile smell of the hospital. The wide range of feelings, and that raw emotion which takes away clear thinking and replaces it with dull pain and mental fatigue.

And how about the brutal conversations? When the doctor is attempting to give the slightest glimmer of hope, but you know that he doesn't believe your little girl is going to survive, or when the nursing staff and attendants are trying their best to prepare you for the worst possible outcome. Those are cruel conversations. Cruel. And yet, so many have it so much worse. And, this isn't a comparison. This is perspective. It's all suffering and it can all be cruel.

Suffering isn't only the trauma and life-threatening moments we've endured. Sometimes, the cruelty of suffering is simply the repeated blood draws and lab work that our girls' medicine regimen requires, to ensure they aren't risking any long-term organ damage from the chemicals they ingest. How do you explain to a non-verbal child with the cognitive awareness of a nine-month-old baby that the nurse has to stick them with a needle, but it's for her good? What about the repeated efforts to find the vein, only to miss and miss and miss, ultimately either sending us home without getting the needed labs or calling a care flight nurse to assist, in hopes that they will have better luck finding the right place to try? How do you explain that to our girls, while they're crying and sweating from fighting while the procedure takes place? It seems cruel.

How about the indignity that comes with helplessness? Our girls are thirteen and ten years old respectively, and both diapered, requiring total personal care. Very few places are equipped to accommodate diaper changes safely and discreetly, which leaves parents and families with awkward and unsanitary choices. This is only more complicated once puberty has arrived, complicating the personal care for both the girls and for us as their caregivers.

Even the more progressive public restrooms, which have changing stations available, are almost always constructed only for babies and are not large enough to accommodate our girls and don't offer any privacy, which is mandatory to preserve their innocence and dignity. On a few occasions, we have resorted to using a bathroom floor while someone stands watch to keep the door closed for privacy, but this is almost always a last resort as it is dirty and completely unsanitary. It's nasty. Most often we're sprawled out in the back of our minivan with one of the children assisting me in holding a full-size blanket as a screen in hopes of providing some privacy and maintaining as much dignity for the girls as we can. We've mastered this technique on road trips and like a NASCAR pit crew, everyone knows their role and I'm proud to say that we can get a full diaper change done in minutes! But I wouldn't want to mislead you either, it's humbling. At times it's humiliating. It can be cruel.

The cruelty of suffering isn't just physical either. It can also be relational. I mentioned earlier in the book that I believe most people who say hurtful things in the midst of someone's suffering did not honestly intend to hurt them. I sincerely believe that. It has been my overwhelming experience that most people simply don't know what to say when someone is hurting, but they think they have to say something, so they will occasionally say the wrong thing instead. David Powlison hit the nail on the head here when he wrote, "Suffering often brings a doubled pain. In the first place, there is 'the problem' itself—perhaps sickness or poverty, betrayal or bereavement. That is hard enough. But it is often compounded by a second problem. Other people, even well-meaning, often respond poorly to sufferers. Sufferers are often misunderstood, or meddled with, or ignored. These reactions add relational and psychological isolation to the original problem." [39]

In their book, *Why, O God?*, authors Larry Waters and Roy Zuck give needed wisdom on this, when they write, "The disturbing *why* question is haunting wherever suffering and disability rear their heads. 'Why did this happen to me?' 'Why doesn't God heal me?' 'Why didn't God protect me from this?' In light of the Bible's presentation of the complexity of the causes of suffering, pastoral caregivers need not be frustrated by their inability to provide authoritative answers about causes. As in the case of biblical events, answers to the *why* question may remain buried in the unrevealed wisdom of God. As a result, caregivers would do well to anticipate a ministry of listening to unending questions without giving answers that are completely satisfying. Appreciation of the mystery of God's work in and through suffering brings with it a humility of service and a proper pause in providing answers." [40]

I have arrived at this opinion based not only upon my own experiences in our family and with our girls, but in my pastoral ministry as well, through the observations of watching people engage and interact with others who are hurting around them. Mary and I have often teased that we would want to write a book entitled, *Stupid Things People Say to Help*. But I don't believe that book needs to be written, as cathartic as it might be for us to get out. I also don't know that our commentary with each of the conversations we recalled would be appropriate.

If, however, it was to be written, I would include the story of the man who came up to me following a men's event where I had just finished preaching. In my sermon, I used a brief illustration on suffering and trials and I shared a moment from a recent doctor's appointment with one of the girls. This older gentleman approached and kindly thanked me for my message and then asked me if, when I said "special needs" to describe my daughter, did I mean she was "retarded." Somewhat shocked, I said, "Yes, she has severe cognitive and physical disabilities." He went on to explain that he understood and had a grandson who was dyslexic and was having a difficult time learning to read. I smiled and nodded and moved on, but I was shocked and hurt. I don't tell that story to make fun of that man, I honestly don't believe he knew how insensitive his phrasing of that question and comparative analysis truly was. I also don't in any way diminish the significance and sincerity of dyslexia or any learning difference, they are all legitimate and challenging and painfully cruel in their own way. Suffering is common to all. The specifics of suffering differ as much as the people who experience them. I simply share that story as one personal example of cruelty in suffering through relationships. I'll offer one more.

When Libby was about three years old and Mary was pregnant with Hannah, we were fortunate enough to get Libby's first wheelchair. It was a great wheelchair. It was gray with pink trim and was customizable so that it could be adjusted as Libby grew. It was sturdy and would fit in the back of Mary's car, even though it wasn't totally collapsible like a baby stroller. One day while pushing Libby in it, another young mom came over admiring the wheelchair and began to ask Mary about it. Mary bragged on how great it was and how much we loved the size and durability and then politely explained that it actually wasn't a stroller, which the other mother had assumed, but was a wheelchair for our daughter Libby (who was sitting in it at the time). The other woman replied, "Well, do you know if I can get one for my normal kid?" Fortunately, Mary had another friend nearby who heard the conversation and to this day I'm convinced that the

Holy Spirit kicked in there as well and that friend grabbed Mary by the arm, and without responding they walked away. Cruel, right?

Perhaps we would all do well to remember the words of James, *"Know this, my beloved brothers: let every person be quick to hear, slow to speak, slow to anger; for the anger of man does not produce the righteousness of God"* (James 1:19–20 ESV). I think for those of us who feel compelled to say something to someone who we know is experiencing a season of suffering, we are best served if we can remember the first part of James's advice: *"...let every person be quick to hear, slow to speak."* You see, I think we often get the order wrong. Albeit with really good intentions and a motive that is pure, I think sometimes we are quick to speak and slow to listen.

However, because suffering is common to everyone, be reminded that all of you who read this will be granted opportunity upon opportunity to speak into the lives of those who are suffering. So, I would remind you that James says we should listen carefully. You might have an idea of what you want to say, that you are convinced they need to hear, but listen carefully because that might be all you need to do. And when you do speak, go slowly. Don't feel like everything has to be said or that you are the one who has to say it. The Proverbs warn us about the danger of quick speech. *"Do you see a man who is hasty in his words? There is more hope for a fool than for him"* (Proverbs 29:20 ESV). I'm writing this encouragement from experience. I have learned this the hard way, both as the offender and as the offended. I've heard it said that the formula for wise counsel is (1) prayer, (2) listening, and (3) response.

Randy Alcorn gives practical, biblical wisdom on this subject of our speaking into another's suffering when he writes, "Jesus wept over the death of Lazarus and his bereaved sisters, Mary and Martha, not because he lost perspective, but because he had perspective. Death is an enemy, as is the suffering and disability that precedes death. God hates it. So should we. We are to rejoice for the coming day when God promises no more death and suffering. Such rejoicing can fully coexist with mourning great loss. We should avoid spiritual-sounding comments that minimize suffering, such as 'God must have loved your son very much to take him home this young.' Parents who hear this will say, 'Then I wish God loved him less.' A friend told me that when her child died, a well-meaning woman assured her it was 'for the best.' My friend, a committed believer, said, 'I wanted to tell her to shut up.'

"Don't say to a person whose child has died, 'I know what you're going through; my mom died.' It may have been difficult for you, it may help you empathize to a degree, but it's not the same. Those who suffer loss need our love and encouragement. They do not need us to minimize or erase their pain through comparison; they need to feel and express it fully." [41]

I counsel people who engage with those in suffering to usually say *only* three things: (1) **I'm so sorry**—I think it is critically important that we acknowledge sadness and grief over whatever it is that they are suffering. (2) **This is awful**—Every sufferer should be validated in their suffering with the acknowledgment that whatever they are facing and enduring is bad for them. (3) **I love you**—The unconditional Gospel-reminder that we love and support one another in the midst of suffering is Christ's work in and through us.

And as we reflect on that Scripture from James Chapter 1, I believe he wasn't only talking to those of us who tend to speak before we think. Actually, Mary and I would do well to remember the wise warning he offers in the second part of his advice: "*...slow to anger; for the anger of man does not produce the righteousness of God.*" So, the next time someone says something hurtful to us, we would do well to remember that we need to be slow to arrive at our anger. It isn't wrong for us to be hurt, that is natural, and James makes no comment against that. It's when our anger is born out of that hurt or anything else that it becomes dangerous and could lead us to sin. I confess to you that I have struggled with this. I haven't always responded apart from anger and I have certainly held thoughts that were rooted in anger. But the formula for wise counsel works in response to: (1) prayer, (2) listening, and (3) response. These are just some of the challenges of suffering and the cruelty which often accompanies them.

Of course, cruelty in suffering isn't only in the physical or the relational, but there's a terribly emotional element that goes along with it too. When emotions are driven from one test to the next, from one hospitalization to the next, from one disappointment to the next, it can be emotionally exhausting. We are *always* the family stared at in public. There isn't a restaurant we visit where some furniture doesn't have to be moved to accommodate our family as we are seated. I am so used to apologizing to others as we carefully navigate wheelchairs past their tables on the way to ours that I don't even think about it anymore.

Our girls both wear bibs over their shirts because they drool and chew on teething toys *a lot.* They make strange noises and when they get excited sometimes they will flap their arms or shake their head and wiggle in their chairs. Of course, we think it is adorable, but we also admit that if you're not used to it, it is abnormal and can seem weird. I totally get that. It would have been strange to me as well before God blessed us with Libby and Hannah who taught me to love it.

When we're at the mall or at a store most people look with pity, some look with concern, and a few look in disgust. One time, as we were leaving a restaurant, a woman wondered out loud to her table of friends, "What's wrong with those parents? That little girl is far too old to still use a pacifier!" I'll admit it, both Libby and Hannah (ages thirteen and ten respectively) still enjoy a pacifier. There are multiple medical and sensory-related reasons I could give to explain this but let me just summarize as their dad and tell you that we allow it because they both enjoy it. Remember, they are cognitively about nine months of age, even though they have the physical body type of their actual ages. Nevertheless, this comment infuriated me and when I calmed down, I realized that my anger was ultimately just hurt feelings. Not my own but hurt for my girls who didn't even know they were being judged and looked down upon. It felt cruel.

Likewise, anytime people attempt to explain their foolish or immature behavior by labeling it "retarded", I cringe in hurt and wince in anger. And yet ... before my girls, I could have easily been the one using that word as that type of adjective, because I was just ignorant enough not to know any better. But now, on this side of things, it hurts. It's mean. It's cruel. And that cruelty has resulted in an overflow of emotions on so many occasions.

I have cried in doctors' offices, emergency rooms, hospital rooms, NICUs, PICUs, therapy sessions, school ARDs, school programs, Mary's arms, both my brothers' shoulders, my friends' shoulders, my home, my office, my truck on Interstate 20, the shower, and a bunch of other places I can't remember. I'll remind you, emotions are God-given and not to be ignored completely or submitted to entirely. They are to be handed over to God for processing. I don't ever want to diminish how hard suffering can be. Yes, life with our daughters is an unbelievable blessing. Truly, more than I could have ever imagined it would be. But it is also hard. Really, really hard.

Within some Christian circles I have encountered along the way, there seems to be a way of thinking which communicates that, if you struggle with suffering as a Christ-follower, there must be something wrong with you. That is not true, and it has been terribly frustrating to deal with that lie on the occasions when it has been presented to me. I have encountered this dishonest thought in our personal journey and I have witnessed it in my pastoral ministry as well. Suffering isn't natural. Suffering is not what God created in the beginning. It is a by-product and consequence of sin and the broken condition of our fallen world. Therefore, it is okay to struggle. It is okay to admit that suffering is hard, and it does not make you a bad Christian or less of a Christian simply because the struggle in suffering is real. After all, cruelty in suffering is just, well … cruel.

But what about those huge questions I alluded to earlier? The ones every pastor is asked and every sufferer, therefore every person, wrestles with at one time or another. Do you remember? "Why do bad things happen to good people?" or "If God is good, why is there bad and evil in the world at all?" These questions are theological. They are biblical. They are serious and worthy of a thoughtful, seriously biblical response, so I will do my best to provide that. And while many others who are much smarter and more eloquent and better equipped to answer these questions have done so in a number of ways already, I will do my best to offer my answer, weaving our story into the response, so you will better know why it matters so much to me.

Think back to our story from John Chapter 9, and the man born blind. First, let's think about this theologically in its broadest sense, as it relates to the suffering of all humanity. Do you remember how Jesus promised God's work in the man born blind? I believe one of the ways we see God's workmanship in suffering is that suffering reveals a brokenness for which God alone can heal. All suffering points to all brokenness. Physical suffering says our bodies are broken and only Jesus can restore. Emotional suffering says our minds are broken and only Jesus can renew. Relational suffering says our communities are broken and only Jesus can reconcile. Spiritual suffering says our souls are broken and only Jesus can redeem.

Alcorn gives a good theological explanation of suffering and evil when he says, "Secondary evils point to primary evil, reminding us that humanity, guilty of sin, deserves suffering. Secondary evil, the direct and indirect consequences of primary evil, provokes our indignation. Why do innocent people suffer? God hates the primary evils we commit, while we hate the secondary evils (consequences) God determines or permits.

"As humans, however, we all stand guilty. Although many secondary evils befall us even when we have not directly committed a sin that causes them, we would not have to deal with secondary evils if we didn't belong to a sinful race. Short-term suffering serves as a warning and foretaste of eternal suffering. Without a taste of Hell, we would not see its horrors nor feel much motivation to do everything possible to avoid it. Hence, the secondary evil of suffering can get our attention and prompt us to repent of our primary moral evil." [42]

That's why Jesus used this man's physical ailment to reveal a greater spiritual need. I mean think about the Gospel implications in this text. We are ALL born spiritually blind. On our own, we are unable to seek truth and discover God's salvation. But, by the grace and mercy of God and through our faith in Jesus Christ, we can all see and experience the salvation of God and the forgiveness of sin. This blind man's physical condition was used by God as His workmanship to reveal the greater spiritual need. This is what Paul says, when he writes to the church in Corinth: *"And even if our gospel is veiled, it is veiled to those who are perishing. In their case the god of this world has blinded the minds of the unbelievers, to keep them from seeing the light of the gospel of the glory of Christ, who is the image of God. For what we proclaim is not ourselves, but Jesus Christ as Lord, with ourselves as your servants for Jesus' sake. For God, who said, 'Let light shine out of darkness,' has shone in our hearts to give the light of the knowledge of the glory of God in the face of Jesus Christ"* (2 Corinthians 4:3–6 ESV).

Friend, let me assure you, **if you are looking at your suffering and at your season of trial for the purposes of finding meaning, significance, and hope ONLY in the immediate and temporary reality of this life now, you will miss the greatest evidence of God's workmanship and the glory that is the Gospel.** Jesus has come to deliver us from all the brokenness of our sin and suffering for eternity, even if the relief we are asking for doesn't happen in the here and now. <u>ALL</u> suffering—yes, all of it—regardless of whether it is understood or not, points to the brokenness in us and around us that God alone can restore.

Author Tim Keller expresses this work of God in the specific tragedy of suffering as central to the Christian faith, when he writes, "The Christian understanding of suffering is dominated by the idea of grace. In Christ, we have received forgiveness, love, and adoption into the family of God. These goods are undeserved, and that frees us from the temptation to feel proud of our suffering. But also is the present enjoyment of those inestimable goods that makes suffering bearable." [43]

Again, this idea of spiritual blindness is something pointed to elsewhere in the Scriptures. When Paul is pleading his case before King Agrippa, and sharing his own story of salvation, he recalls the very words Jesus spoke to him regarding the reality of spiritual blindness that we all suffer from. Listen to Acts 26:16–18: *"But rise and stand upon your feet, for I have appeared to you for this purpose, to appoint you as a servant and witness to the things in which you have seen* *me and to those in which I will appear to you, delivering you from your people and from the Gentiles—to whom I am sending you to <u>open their eyes</u>, so that they may turn from darkness to light and from the power of Satan to God, that they may receive forgiveness of sins and a place among those who are sanctified by faith in me."* Jesus answers the question and uses the example of the man's blindness from birth and subsequent suffering as a platform that reveals God's workmanship from a greater spiritual suffering, a suffering from which Jesus is the only one who can deliver. This is where I find my greatest strength for Libby and Hannah. Jesus lived a life we couldn't live and died a death that we deserve. He rose for our salvation so that we might spend eternity with God. Whether they know they need the forgiveness of God or not, I believe the Bible is clear that Jesus has secured it and Libby and Hannah have received it. That changes everything, even how we see the cruelty of suffering.

Additionally, I want to remind you of a fundamental and foundational Gospel truth that I have learned by navigating our own story of suffering. The subtitle of this book is: *A Father's Perspective on the Theology of Suffering,* and as it relates to suffering, I have shared a great deal of my perspective based upon our experience. I would, however, be remiss if I didn't remind you that I am only one broken father telling you *my* perspective. The power and majesty of the Gospel reveals a perfect heavenly Father who has a perfect perspective on suffering. My girls have suffered and I have watched through broken lenses, but God the Father watched His only Son suffer and He witnessed it with perfectly clear vision. Authors Tada and Estes explain, "God, like a father, doesn't just give advice. He gives himself. He becomes the husband to the grieving widow (Isaiah 54:5). He becomes the comforter to the barren woman (Isaiah 54:1). He becomes the father of the orphaned (Psalm 10:14). He becomes the bridegroom to the single person (Isaiah 62:5). He is the healer to the sick (Exodus 15:26). He is the wonderful counselor to the confused and depressed (Isaiah 9:6).

"This is what you do when someone you love is in anguish; you respond to the plea of their heart by giving them your heart. If you are the One at the center of the universe, holding it together, if everything moves, breathes, and has its being in you, you can do no more than give yourself (Acts 17:28)." [44] This is what makes our faith in Christ and the power of the gospel so significant. As Keller explains, "So, while Christianity never claims to be able to offer a full *explanation* of all God's reasons behind every instance of evil and suffering—it does have a final *answer* to it. That answer will be given at the end of history and all who hear it and see its fulfillment will find it completely satisfying, infinitely sufficient." [45] So we, as followers of Christ, trust what God sees perfectly, when we only see dimly. We rest in what God knows infinitely, when we only understand partially. We hope in what God has done finally, when we only think temporarily.

Dave Furman offers a similar summary explanation when he writes, "In the same way Christians should never get over the incarnation of Jesus. It's surprising that God would come to us. When we are walking through trials of various kinds, we need to remember this truth. God did not leave us alone in this world. The Son of God left heaven and came to earth. He faced incredible pain and suffering Himself to rescue us from our sin and bring us hope in our trials." [46] God knows suffering because as we have seen over and over again, God endured suffering. The worst suffering. And, He did it for you and me to be saved.

But finally, so many of us continue to struggle with this question of how God can allow suffering to happen to the "innocent." Let's deal with that because it is important. We must see that suffering only happened to the truly innocent once. The power and majesty of the Gospel is that God has done for us what we could not do for ourselves because He undeservedly took upon Himself that which was rightly owed to us.

I love the way Joni Eareckson Tada expresses this, when she says, "When I think of all this, it strikes me that these limitations didn't just 'happen' to Jesus in the same way that circumstances 'happen' to you and me. The amazing thing is that Christ *chose* to be handicapped. I can't think of too many people who would actually choose to be disabled. Believe me, I know I wouldn't! There is nothing easy, nothing fun, nothing casual about dealing with a disability. From the very get-go, it's *hard*.

"But Jesus chose to handicap Himself so that you and I might share eternity with Him in bodies that will never stoop, limp, falter, or fail. Jesus chose to experience pain and suffering beyond our imagination in order that you and I would one day walk the streets of heaven whole, happy, and pain free. Jesus chose to die—though that was a daunting task in itself. As C. S. Lewis wrote, Jesus "was so full of life that when He wished to die He had to 'borrow death from others.' But borrow it He did, taking it unto Himself, yielding up His life, so that you and I might pass through death's shadow and live forever. Yes, while I'm alive here on earth, I am called to endure a handicap. But how could I be anything other than grateful and content? I'm in the best company of all." [47]

Think about this. Jesus was and is innocent, but He died like the guilty. *"Since then we have a great high priest who has passed through the heavens, Jesus, the Son of God, let us hold fast our confession. For we do not have a high priest who is unable to sympathize with our weaknesses, but one who in every respect has been tempted as we are, yet without sin"* (Hebrews 4:14–15 ESV). I understand the sentiment of wanting to argue for the innocence of someone who is young, especially like a baby, a small child, or someone with a cognitive disability like our girls. I get it. I've done it. It makes sense to me. But that argument is a misunderstanding of genuine innocence. Genuine innocence is to be without any wrong, to have complete and perfect purity. And no person, regardless of age or ability, can lay claim to that, except Jesus. The Bible says our sin is in our nature, inherited from our first father Adam. *"Therefore, just as sin came into the world through one man, and death through sin, and so death spread to all men because all sinned"* (Romans 5:12 ESV). But Jesus wasn't from Adam. He was divinely conceived by the Holy Spirit, directly given to Mary and therefore He escaped the nature of sin which plagues the rest of us.

What's more, not only was Jesus born sinless, but He lived sinlessly. He was perfect, and yet ... died as though He were not. For us. *"For our sake he made him to be sin who knew no sin, so that in him we might become the righteousness of God"* (Corinthians 5:21 ESV).

Randy Alcorn explains by saying, "It's one thing to suffer terribly, another to *choose* to suffer terribly. Evil and suffering formed the crucible in which God demonstrated His love to mankind. What is good about 'Good Friday'? Why isn't it called 'Bad Friday'? Because out of the appallingly bad came what was inexpressibly good. And the good trumps the bad, because though the bad was temporary, the good is eternal. God's love comes to us soaked in divine blood. One look at Jesus—at His incarnation and the redemption He provided us—should silence the argument that God has withdrawn to some far corner of the universe where He keeps His hands clean and maintains His distance from human suffering. God does not merely empathize with our sufferings. He actually suffers. Jesus is God. What Jesus suffered, God suffered." [48]

So, when your suffering is cruel, let that remind you of the cruelty of the cross. The only place in all of history where the innocent truly suffered. And in His suffering for our sins, He made a way for our suffering to end, forever. Suffering is real. Suffering can be cruel. Call it what it is and give thanks and praise to God through Christ who has overcome it all.

Chapter 10

"COMPLETE"

We have developed a tradition around the family dinner table at our house. It has honestly become one of my favorite things that we do. In an effort to engage our kids in conversation, beyond the usual "How was your day?" followed by a series of grunts and eye rolls, and for the conversation to be as redemptive as possible in which everyone is required to participate, the tradition was started. On most nights, we play a game around the dinner table called, "Pit and Peak." The premise of the game is simple. Every person shares the worst part of their day, the pit, and then they share the best part of their day, the peak. Each person can give as much detail about each part as they wish and everyone else is invited to ask questions or celebrate victories or offer words of encouragement if and when they are needed. It is usually lighthearted and gives plenty of fodder for teasing and picking at one another, but I feel like I should confess that on more than one occasion it has included tears or ended in tears. For the most part, it is a lot of fun and an easy way for us to navigate dinner conversation easily.

Our youngest daughter, eight-year-old Campbell, loves to pick the batting order and make the rules as to who goes first and who goes last. Sometimes she says youngest to oldest, other times she says smallest to tallest and occasionally she mixes it up with a random order that only she gets to decide. Any way you slice it, I can assure you she's always going first. Additionally, we will also mix up our "Pit and Peak" game by adding mandated accents to be spoken by each person as they are describing their personal pits and peaks of that day. My default is a British accent, which I'm quite proud of. My daughter Kathryn will usually draw on that one as well, while my son Coleman almost always chooses to travel a little further south and brings a terrible Australian accent to the game. Campbell doesn't have any accents yet, her best attempts are simply to raise the volume of her talking and Mary is a huge party pooper and usually refuses to attempt any accent at all. It's a fun, wheels-off few minutes around our dinner table to be sure, but there is always laughter and everyone gets to share. We are each invited, if only for a few minutes, into one another's world for the best and worst parts of that particular day. I love playing "Pit and Peak" with my family.

In this chapter, I'd like to invite you to dinner with us. Only instead of playing "Pit and Peak" traditionally, I've asked several of our family members to simply share their own thoughts, feelings, experiences, and struggles from the journey we've been on with our girls. I think hearing the perspective of other family members will be helpful and might give an even broader and clearer picture as to how God has used and is using our girls to impact, change, shape, and bless our lives. Let's go tallest to smallest, which means I'm up first.

How do I begin explaining all the ways my girls, Libby and Hannah, have impacted my life? I honestly don't know that I can do justice to this deep desire that I have to speak of the blessings my girls have brought me. I've taken the majority of this book to explain the hardship that comes with their suffering, but it would be entirely incomplete to ignore all of the incredible ways I have experienced and am still experiencing the grace of God through the lives of these two little girls. But, in an effort to write something here, I'll give five thoughts on what I have seen God do thus far.

First, I am very aware that each day we have with these girls is precious. In our fast-paced world of always looking toward what's next, I have grown more keenly aware of the treasure and the gift of life. Because I believe all life is created by God, then this new appreciation for the value of life, the brevity of life, and the joy that comes in life, all help stir my affections for God as a worship-inducing by-product. Of course, all parents would agree that all days with all children are precious. But, given the original prognosis of losing our girls by the age of two, and yet for no reason other than God's grace still having them today, it makes our time together so much more valuable and cherished. Each day with them is a gift. We are living on borrowed time, but borrowed only from our doctors and not from our God.

Second, the journey with our girls has deepened my trust in the Lord and therefore strengthened my prayer life with the Lord. I have not always been a disciplined person. I have not always maintained discipline in my physical health (i.e., diet and exercise) or in my spiritual health (i.e., prayer and Bible reading). But, just like when a doctor gives you a dire prognosis if your health doesn't improve, mandating radical lifestyle changes to promote it, in the same way, God can use trials and suffering to motivate radical spiritual changes in your life as well. And I have found that because of the rarity of our girls' diagnosis and then subsequently all of the unknowns that come from treating the symptoms and complications that result from it, I have been forced to rely upon the Lord for grace, healing, and supernatural provision where medicine and men were unable to ease my angst. Do we still use medicine and glean the wisdom of man? Yes, absolutely! But are we finding our ultimate comfort in what that will provide our girls in the end? No, absolutely not!

I'm challenged by the honest words of author Mark Vroegop, when he writes, "I wonder how many believers stop speaking to God about their pain. Disappointed by unanswered prayers or frustrated by out-of-control circumstances, these people wind up in a spiritual desert unable—or—refusing to talk to God. This silence is a soul killer. Maybe you are one of those who've given God the silent treatment. Maybe you just don't know what to say. Perhaps there's a particular issue or struggle that you just can't talk to God about. It feels too painful. I hope you'll be encouraged to start praying again. Or perhaps you have a friend who is really struggling in grief. Maybe this person prays for some things that make you uncomfortable—even wince. But before you jump in too quickly and hush his or her prayer, remember that at least your friend is praying. It's a start. Prayers of lament take faith." 49

When the doctors don't know what to do and the outcome seems bleak, prayer has been the greatest treatment plan I've been prescribed. Libby and Hannah have taught me to pray with reckless abandon. They have taught me to forsake the insecurities of how it might look to pray when we begin a meeting at our local public school about the girls' educational plan, or in a pre-op waiting room handing off to anesthesia, or in an ambulance on the way to Dallas, or in the middle of the night when they can't tell you what hurts, or at a laboratory when, after four failed attempts, they still can't find a vein. My girls have taught me that I can call out to God in prayer anytime for anything. They have taught me to pray when everything is going wrong and when everything is going right—when they are sick and the outlook is grim and when they are healthy and thriving in their daily routine. God has used the girls to deepen my trust in Him and has granted me the desire for more and more prayer conversations with Him.

Third, the girls have forever shaped our family for the better. I am so blessed to watch Mary up close as she serves our girls tirelessly and selflessly on a daily basis. She always meets their needs before her own and tends to their personal care and well-being in the most Christ-like way. As a testimony of how God uses my bride, I cannot tell you how many doctors and nurses have commented on the girls' generally good health or their exceptional hygiene, or their joy and contentment. And with each compliment, it is almost always loaded with great surprise and appreciation. You see, because special needs persons are often so challenging to care for, much of the care they receive is not always great. Tragically, this is what many doctors and nurses are more accustomed to seeing. But not our girls and my Mary is responsible for that. She's a champion, truly.

Our other three children, Kathryn, Coleman, and Campbell have also been greatly transformed and shaped by our girls, their sisters. Watching each one love their sisters in ways that are unique and special to them blesses me as the dad to all five in ways that are tough to describe here.

I'm choking back tears as I think about how Kathryn cares for Libby and Hannah like a maternal nurse, with instincts toward love and care that are obviously gifts from the Lord. She also is fiercely protective of both girls in the most incredible ways and I love that she will not tolerate anyone being rude or unkind to them. Kathryn has been exposed to some of the worst parts of our journey, including a few of our most challenging moments with these girls, and I am grateful that Jesus has used those events to shape and mold her into a Gospel warrior for the marginalized, helpless, and often overlooked in our world.

Coleman, too, has been shaped into a fiercely loyal protector of his little sisters. He is an unbelievable servant who is constantly running to grab things we've forgotten and wiping the drool from their mouths or helping unload and set up their wheelchairs, all while moving ahead with our family rhythm and schedule. Coleman is adamant that these girls be as much a part of "normal" as anyone else's siblings might. Coleman is sensitive to protecting the girls' dignity and he is very playful with both sisters as only a big brother can be.

Campbell has also been a joy to watch engage with Libby and Hannah. She will tell you, if you ask, that Hannah is her best friend. They grew up like babies together and Hannah was actually in a baby crib longer than Campbell, so they are naturally very close to one another. Campbell still gets in bed with her sisters to watch YouTube videos of Mickey Mouse, or to play the *Frozen II* soundtrack and sing along, or to watch *Shrek* and laugh out loud at all of the inappropriate bodily noises celebrated throughout the film. She has slumber parties in the bed with Hannah and will stay up talking to them both. She has never known life apart from these two girls and so everything for her is normative, including the hundreds of doctors' appointments she has gone to with us. Campbell thinks her sisters are awesome and she wouldn't understand it if anyone did not. I am grateful for this innocence and I think we could all benefit from a little more of Campbell's perspective on those who are different from us.

My family has been forever shaped in the most positive ways by Libby and Hannah. And Libby and Hannah have been forever shaped in the most positive ways by our family. I would have never known how God was going to use the Bales family dynamic to mold each one of us individually into who He created us to be together, but it is a joy to watch unfold.

Fourth, I am so grateful to God for the ways He has used our girls to shape our extended family and friends. My brothers, Jayson and Neil, each have a close relationship with their nieces for different, but special reasons. Libby likes that Jayson has always held her and talked with her and made her a priority to him. Hannah likes Neil's beard and that he doesn't mind if she pulls it or tries to eat it because it's a sensory toy to her. Likewise, their spouses and children are all incredibly kind to our girls. When our extended families get together, on both sides of our family, our girls are right in the thick of things and everyone is taking turns holding them and talking to them and teasing them. They are just a part of our family dynamic and I credit our entire family for their Christ-like acceptance and love of Libby and Hannah.

Our parents have also been a tremendous blessing to us. Watching them change and grow through the experiences they have shared with their granddaughters has been a joy to see. Our parents have been very supportive, clocking hundreds of hours of babysitting during hospital stays, and offering hundreds of hours in prayer asking for God's provision for their lives. I am so grateful for how God has shaped our family through the gift of our girls.

Our friends too have been forever changed by Libby and Hannah. Watching other families, who may or may not have much experience with individuals with special needs, engage and love our girls is so much fun for me! I love seeing how our girls are talked to and treated in the most normative way by other moms and dads and kids who love them because they love us. I have also seen God use our girls to broaden many of those families' understanding and appreciation for disability ministry, including using our girls' story as a catalyst for founding and funding that ministry in other settings for other people. So many of our friends have displayed patience with us as we move slower when we go out to eat or on a vacation. So many friends have stood watch during prayer vigils, given hours and hours in hospital visitations, thousands and thousands of dollars, and dozens and dozens of meals all in the name of Christ's love for our family because God used our girls. Paul Tripp beautifully summarizes this gift of the biblical community when he writes, "Yes, it's true that the God of all comfort sends His ambassadors of comfort into your life. They're sent to make God's invisible presence, protection, strength, wisdom, love, and grace visible. So welcome his ambassadors. Be open to their insight and counsel. Confess your needs so that God's helpers can minister to those needs. Live like you really do believe that your walk through hardship is a community project, and be ready for the good things God will do." [50]

Fifth and finally, I am forever grateful to see how God has used our girls to shape our churches. From the church we attended when Libby was born, who filled the hospital surgical waiting room during heart surgery and have subsequently added a vibrant special needs ministry to serve other families like ours, to the church where I first served on staff and where I serve again today, which had a vision for special needs ministry before it was as widely accepted and as understood as it is now. Our church was on the forefront of this Gospel ministry and our family has been and is being shaped by the influence it has on us and so many others even now. And for our church in East Texas, this body of believers were literally the hands of feet of Christ to us during the worst moments of our life. They stood watch and in the gap in so many ways, they can't all be recounted. This church has a vibrant special needs ministry on both of its campuses today and hundreds of people are impacted either by the ministry as recipients or through the ministry as servants. I love how God has broadened in each one of our church families a perspective on suffering and the Kingdom of God. I am humbled and honored that He has used Libby and Hannah Bales to do so much of it. These are just some of the blessings the girls have brought to me!

Next up, my wife, Mary:

*As I think about my journey with the Lord, there are a few
defining moments. There are moments when I know that
the Lord was present. That He was working in our midst.
Honestly, most of these moments occur after a season of great
confusion and feelings of abandonment.*

*This is how I would describe the first few months of Libby's life.
In the beginning, I was confused, sad, and doubting. How could
God do this to our girl? What was He up to? How was I to
respond to this "new normal" when everything felt so abnormal?
I was angry. I looked around and thought that we had done
everything right. We had surrendered ALL to Him and now we
were walking through this unbelievable suffering. I remember
thinking, "We are not the special needs family—this does not
define us." That was true. I tell people all the time that our
family had a story before Libby and God has only continued that
story. However, we ARE a special needs family. I remember
very clearly surrendering to this. It wasn't easy. I remember
thinking, "Okay, God ... this is where the rubber meets the
road." This is where I have to truly decide if I believe all that
I said I believed before we were thrown this massive curveball. Is
God good? Is He sovereign? Is He loving? Can I trust Him? The
short answer to all of those questions is, "YES." I never want to
minimize the process that led me to that answer. I will tell you
that He has been so faithful. He has used His Spirit, His people,
and His Word to move me to this answer.*

*I cannot count the number of times that I have heard God speak
to my spirit, reminding me that He is there. Reminding me who
He is and who I am in Him. He has prompted me to serve others
who are in the ditch. He has convicted me to be patient for those*

who are grieving. He has encouraged me to walk in my calling
as a wife and mother.

I cannot count the number of times that I was in the ditch and,
with patience and great care, someone has come to sit beside me
in the ditch. Someone was patient while I grieved and processed.
God has used His people to love and minister to our family in
ways that we can never repay or express. We have been prayed
for, fed, visited, and loved in so many countless ways. Our
community of believers has always stepped up. We have had
a rare glimpse of The Church at work. Since we lived in the
Dallas area for twelve years and then moved to East Texas, we
had the beautiful picture of our local churches working together
to love and serve us. Every single time we were sent to Dallas
for a hospitalization, the church in East Texas was there to pray
us off and provide for those in our home. When we arrived at
the ER, the church in Dallas was there to greet us, praying and
providing for our needs while in the hospital. The Church and
her fellowship are a beautiful piece of our story.

God's Word—wow. I think about my journey before the girls.
My limited understanding of God's ability to speak and move
and act. I read stories in the Bible and wondered if He would do
the same for me? As Connor shared about our study of John 9,
God also engraved a Scripture on my heart. It has become my life
verse. You probably won't find it on a coffee mug, but the truth
of it has changed my life! "I have said these things to you, that in
me you may have peace. In the world you will have tribulation.
But take heart; I have overcome the world" (John 16:33 ESV). As
I think about this verse, I am grateful for all that He has taught
me. In this world, broken and fallen, we WILL have tribulation.
He never promised us an easy life, He never promised that life
in Christ was easy. You only have to read the New Testament to

see the lives of His disciples. I began to wrap my mind around the fact that I had a terrible theology of suffering. I believed that my faith and my dedication to the things of God would exempt me from the brokenness of this world, and the brokenness of my family. When I began to see that no one is exempt, I could begin to try to understand where hope is found.

For believers, we have an eternal hope that Jesus has come to deliver us into the right relationship with God. He has overcome the world — that means everything that you and I go through, He has already overcome it. We have not ... that is why there is grief and pain. That is why we are angry and sad. Sometimes, we can feel overcome by our grief, sadness, anger, and questions. Here is what I have learned, God can handle all of that. So many times, we try to fake it with God. We are surrounded by pithy statements and terrible theology that tell us that "God will never give us more than we can handle," or "If you have enough faith, healing will come." **Here is the truth, God always gives us more than we can handle because He loves us enough to engage in our suffering.**

I'm encouraged by what Randy Alcorn writes, when he says, "Suffering is limited. It could be far worse. Suffering is temporary. It could last far longer. Suffering, as we've seen, produces some desirable good. It can make us better people, and it can reveal God's character in ways that bring Him glory and bring us good. God can see all the ultimate results of suffering; we can see only some. When we see more, in His presence we will forever praise Him for it. He calls upon us to trust Him and begin that praise now." [51]

2 Corinthians 1:9 says, *"Indeed, we felt that we had received the sentence of death. But that was to make us rely not on*

ourselves but on God who raises the dead." He wants us to rely on Him! So, slowly, over time, I began to rely on Him. When doctors could not give adequate answers or explanations, I began to rely on Him. I began to trust His Word. In His grace and mercy, through some of the most painful and difficult circumstances in my life, He softened me. He was there. He was patient, loving, and consistent. His Word taught me that there is NOTHING that I will ever experience that He has not already overcome on the cross. So, whatever it is—a financial woe, broken relationship, devastating diagnosis—He has overcome it all. This does not dissolve the pain, anger, and sadness, but it does refocus my thoughts from fear to praise, thanking Him for overcoming all that I cannot. When I feel overcome by emotion or circumstance, I'm thankful that He is not. He defeated those things when He went to Calvary. I have learned that He is big enough to handle my grief. I can cry out to Him, I can question and doubt, I can be angry and tell Him about it—He already knows. Why do we try to fake it? He is so big, and all of our emotions are acceptable to Him. He wants us to rely on Him. How can I rely on Him when I am not honest with Him?

So, remember when I said that "the rubber met the road"? This was a beautiful time where I felt the Lord's presence and peace. He gently guided me and was patient with my immaturity. He showed me that it is in the valley where we need the Shepherd the most.

And now, our oldest daughter, Kathryn:

Having Libby and Hannah as sisters has been a very challenging, but also an incredible, experience. They have each taught me many different things that I would like to share with you. Two of the main things that I have learned from having Libby and Hannah are compassion and tenderness. This was revealed to me in the pit of 2018 when Hannah was ill.

When Hannah was first prescribed the new seizure medicine, which created all her complications, I was very angry. I thought that the doctors didn't care about her and that she was "just another patient." And as her medicine started to kick in, she took a turn for the worse and her health was only declining. She was not only having seizures, but she was sleeping all the time and was rarely smiling anymore. She was still Hannah, but she was not MY Hannah as I knew her to be. As I saw a decrease in her health, I neglected to see a change in my attitude, but it was obvious to everyone, except me. I was no longer just angry at this point; I was now infuriated.

One day, this all changed. In March of that same year, she crashed. My mom was out of town which made things even harder on our family because she is our balance among all the chaos. However, with my mom not there, my dad asked me to go with him to the Emergency Room. Not knowing the emotional toll it would take on me, I agreed. When we were in the car, I was sitting in the front with my dad while Hannah was in the back. But during the drive, Hannah was so unstable I climbed in the back to make sure she stayed awake. When we got to the hospital, I was terrified. We rushed Hannah in there only to hear, "Mr. Bales, this is bad you might need to call your wife." I was at a loss for words. Watching Hannah struggle to breathe right in front of me killed me. I wanted to do something but there was nothing I could do, but sit, watch, and pray. While the doctors struggled to get Hannah intubated, I was in the hallway calling my neighbor and my mom, struggling to get out my words.

The nurses and doctors moved Hannah from the regular patient room to trauma, because she was still not intubated, and she was struggling to breathe. After she had been in the trauma room, an emergency room doctor who is also our close family friend, came in from his son's soccer game (in street clothes) and was able to get Hannah intubated. After he got her intubated there was a more assured hope for her life. The doctors still insisted she be care-flighted to Dallas as soon as possible. With this in mind, my dad had a family friend come and pick me up from the ER and take me home. Not knowing if I was going to see Hannah again, I was scared.

*After multiple days of prayer, fear, and love from friends and family, there was less of a fear for Hannah's life. I was still so emotional but was able to focus more clearly and serve my family as much as possible. With Hannah being in the hospital and my parents there with her, I felt lonely, I missed being with my whole family. She was in the PICU for five weeks, but I promise it was an eternity. After those five weeks, when Hannah came home, I noticed a change in myself. I wasn't angry anymore. I got to peek behind the curtain just enough to see that the doctors aren't giving up on her and that she isn't "just another patient", the love that the nurses showed her was unbelievable, and the way the church family ministered and blessed our family was so generous and overwhelming in all the best ways. **Hannah going through such a tough season of suffering showed me the love of God and how He is so gracious to us.** Because of my sisters, I am more compassionate and tender.*

Not only have Hannah and Libby taught me tenderness, but they also taught me to be aware of my surroundings. Like my brother, I will never let a door shut on anybody because of the numerous times I have run ahead to grab the door for a wheelchair. Not only that but if you don't know me, I have a bit of a scrappy personality and that is easily seen if people are making fun of others, especially those who can't stand up for themselves. I don't like it when people use the words "retard" or "retarded" as a common "funny" adjective to describe their friends. My sisters have allowed me to see that everyone has equal value and not one person should be degraded no matter what may be going on in their lives.

They have also shown me how to love the least of these. I have the amazing opportunity almost every year to go and serve at a camp for families with disabilities and be a one-on-one camp counselor for a child with a disability. I count it one of my greatest blessings to see people with special needs or disabilities treated as though they are kings and queens and loved on constantly. It is truly a glimpse of heaven in the way people are loved, served, and cared for the whole week long.

Not only have the girls taught me these things, but they have also been able to give our family many blessings. Because of my girls, we have handicapped parking space, which seems like a small and insignificant thing but when you have 4,000 things to carry and five kids to manage, it makes the world's difference to our family. Not only do we get handicapped parking, but because of Libby and Hannah we have been able to go to Disney World for Libby's "Make A Wish" trip, and we went to Disneyland for Hannah's. This has been such a tremendous blessing and would have never been possible without Libby and Hannah. Libby and Hannah have made such an incredible impact on my life and I am extremely grateful to call them my sisters.

Next up, our son, Coleman:

Life with Libby and Hannah has been like one big roller coaster. There are some highs and lows, but through it all, God has shown me many things. Like for instance, tender-heartedness. If a door is closing, I never let it close on anyone because of all the doors I have opened for our wheelchairs.

*One of the peaks in my life came out of one of the pits. It happened as a result of Hannah's suffering in 2018 when I came to the realization that I was not saved. When Hannah crashed, I was walking the walk. I was praying and doing all the right things, but Hannah kept declining. I thought that Hannah was being punished for something that I had done. So I prayed more and more and harder. But still no increase. So, when she finally got better I thought, "Okay, you didn't mess up and Hannah got better." But then that October she went back to the hospital and was there for about two more weeks. The bad feeling came back. But yet again she came home. December rolled around and on December 5, 2018, God decided to write a story through my life. That night my life was forever changed. **I trusted Christ.** I didn't see why or how something good could come out of Hannah's situation, but that December night I saw clearly why that bad feeling was there—I was praying to a God I knew about but didn't know on a personal level and had no saving relationship with. Now I am eternally grateful that God used an awful situation in my life to turn me from darkness to light.*

Another peak from a pit is that God has shown me how to persevere. I love running, it has become something I really enjoy. But I don't run short races, I do the 800-meter and up—I love the distance. And in distance running, especially the 800-meter, you are basically sprinting for half a mile, so endurance is crucial. But what I've learned is not about physical endurance but mental and spiritual endurance. I learned most of this endurance during the crash phase when Hannah was in the hospital for about eight to ten weeks. Not knowing the outcome, if your little sister will live or die, is terrifying. I can remember nights where I would stay up and hope that I would see either my mom or dad coming home from the hospital. That was the hardest race I have ever run and probably ever will.

Fortunately, because of Libby and Hannah we've been blessed with more peaks like the opportunity to go to both Disney World and Disneyland through "Make A Wish." This was such a blessing because we had spending money, a place to stay, and a "genie pass," which, if you don't know, gets you to the front of the line immediately! But the biggest blessing was the Disney World staff. They went out of their way to make us feel welcome and special. We had several who invited us to private rooms and special quiet rest stops. And that just made me see that the world has good people, you just have to look harder for them. That is both my pit and peak of life with Libby and Hannah.

P.S., My Australian accent is amazing!

Followed by our youngest daughter, Campbell:

Libby and Hannah have taught me to be so crazy! The girls like to laugh and they like funny noises. I like to have sleepovers in their room and I really like to cuddle with them. I like to watch movies in their bed, mostly Disney ones. I like to wrestle with Libby and I really like to push Hannah in her stroller.

*I have learned how to help my mom and dad with my sisters. I can help with bath time and I can unhook their feeding tubes after they've eaten. When the girls are sad I know how to make them happy—I know which toys are their favorites. **God has*** *taught me to be kind in different ways and when God sees the girls I think He thinks they are perfect.*

And next, my mother, Sallye "Granny" Bales:

After I heard that Connor was writing this book and that Libby and Hannah's brother and two sisters were going to be able to express their experiences as siblings to this amazing story, I asked Connor if I could contribute a grandparent's perspective of my relationship with the girls. He has graciously allowed me to share what I call: "my view from the top." By that, I mean when you walk the journey of climbing this life's mountain you reach the top of that mountain when, for some of us, becoming a grandparent occurs. We think of that age as being filled with experience and hopefully God's wisdom that has been gained throughout the journey.

When we became grandparents, neither Granny (me) nor Granddaddy (my late husband) were prepared for having two special needs granddaughters. Our journey with the "view from the top" had not included that. Each one of us had never even been around others who did not have the capacity to walk and talk. In the midst of our broken hearts over this new reality, was the question, "Why, Lord?" Then, fear followed, as our flesh was tempted to think of all the uncertainties and heartbreaks ahead, in the lives of these beyond adorable, sweet, and totally dependent granddaughters.

However, it wasn't long, and Granddaddy was soon cuddling and singing lullabies to each of these precious girls whenever we babysat. I learned to hook up feeding tubes and the two of us saw how God was using these experiences to grow us and expand our horizon in yet another area of our lives. Very quickly we realized that "Libby's world and Hannah's world" are indeed special places! Each place is filled with response, personality, and charm that is unique to Libby Faye and equally unique to Hannah Jane.

Their Granddaddy has gone home to be with Jesus now and I know he will be lovingly waiting with arms open wide whenever these two girls, who are gifts from God placed right in the middle of the Bales bunch, are one day home with Jesus as well. At that time, I can predict that Granddaddy Bales will have tears of joy as he sees Libby and Hannah walk and talk! Some of my favorite family picture memories include Granddaddy holding these two wonderful girls, whom he deeply connected with.

For me, as I continue to lift both Libby and Hannah up to God for healing, I no longer ask, "Why, Lord?" Now, I say, "Thank you, Lord!" I have the blessing of seeing God's strength in Connor and Mary. I see God's support in Kathryn, Coleman, and Campbell in how they love their sisters. I see God's compassion in the Bales' aunts and uncles and cousins. These are precious treasures that a mother, and grandmother, ponders deeply in her heart. **My spiritual journey that has led me to my "view from the top" has forever been blessed and changed by two angel girls ... who do not yet, walk and talk, but will!**

And rounding out the list, Mary's mother, Ellen "Mimi" Pollard:

When Libby was born, Mary and Connor knew right away that there was a problem. She had a hole in the heart and would need open-heart surgery. This was devastating news but not the worst to come. Her heart was fixed and for a moment, ours were as well. We thought all was good. As the months went on, it became evident that there were other problems. Libby was diagnosed with Trisomy 16p.

Dealing with this, Libby's personality was emerging. She knows what she wants and definitely what she doesn't want and lets you know both. I learned early that Libby understands what you say. I was with her one time and I said, "Roll over here and Mimi will pick you up." And she did! She came right over to my feet and I picked her up and we were both happy. I was afraid that she would forget who I was as I am not always there. But she never forgets people. She knows voices. When I come to the house, I can hear her squealing in her room. She wants to see me. Libby loves to be hugged and can give great hugs as well. She likes to play "rough". In fact, after spending time with Libby, others in the family will say,"Oh, you've been to the Libby salon," as she likes to mess up your hair. She does not care for therapy and sometimes doesn't like school. She's social up to a point but then loves being in her bed. She has her favorite movies and songs. I remember one time she helped Mary plan her birthday party by shaking her head yes or no depending on what she wanted. She has learned to say a few words: Mom and Dad. How precious is that? I'm working on getting her to say Mimi.

Libby is an amazing little girl and has spread so much joy! People want Libby to like them and they try hard to make that happen. I love Libby more than I can say and I know she loves me too!

Hannah has the same chromosome disorder as Libby, even though when Mary discovered she was pregnant, the doctors said this would never happen. The disorder is very rare and to have two in the same family just would never happen. But it did! But Libby and Hannah are as different as night and day. Hannah is *pretty much always happy and loves being with people and being held. She loves sitting in her special chair and loves therapy and loves school. It's hard to believe that one disorder can have such different effects on both girls. Hannah is the more fragile of the two. She has had many medical issues—mainly pneumonia. Mary and Connor could both be medical doctors as they know what to do when something goes wrong. Mainly they have found a team of wonderful doctors who work well with them.*

Hannah is so sweet—all still call her sweet little Hannah even though she has grown a lot! She'll always be our sweet little Hannah! Hannah smiles most of the time and chatters away. She can say Mama! I'm working on Mimi with her too!

These are my special and special needs granddaughters. I love how they have taught me to love more than I thought I could. They have taught me to appreciate the small things like a smile or a hug. When either girl starts laughing it seems the world laughs too. Hannah knows how to clap at appropriate times. This has been a joy. They make me and so many others so much happier just by being who they are. I love how they have set the family dynamics. Campbell has grown up saying that Hannah is her best friend. Kathryn is now talking about becoming a surgical nurse. Both Kathryn and Coleman can do most things for the girls. They can hook and unhook the feeding tubes and do many other tasks too. Kathryn and Coleman can lift and carry both girls. If either girl is unhappy, often Coleman is sent in to cheer them up. Life can be so difficult but often it doesn't have to be.

The girls have taught me to take a breath and just enjoy the moment. If I have had a rough day, I stop and think of what kind of day Libby and Hannah have had. Even though they are so restricted by what they can and can't do, they are still happy. I have no right to complain. **They are our special angels put on earth and given to this wonderful family to show us all that we can be better people.** *I remember this often and I do try. Thank you, Libby and Hannah.*

Some days I wish Libby and Hannah could be like every other thirteen and ten-year-old. But then we would miss the Libby and Hannah we have. And as their Mama always says, "You are just perfect!" And they are!

Finally, I want to close this chapter by sharing with you just one last blessing that life with our girls has allowed us to enjoy. I would summarize this blessing as a little bit of heaven on earth. As I have mentioned in other places throughout the book, our girls have given our entire family, extended family, and our friends a passion for special needs ministry that I am confident we would not have except that God placed Libby and Hannah in our family. One of the most wonderful examples of this type of ministry is the amazing life work of long term disability advocate, Joni Eareckson Tada. Since having Libby, Mary and I have only grown in our passion for and blessings from disability ministries, like the one founded by Joni called, Joni and Friends. As we have learned more about her vision and passion for Christ, and its translation into working diligently for decades to serve others with disabilities in His name, Joni has become a hero to me (us) and is someone we look up to and deeply respect.

I think Stephanie Hubach offers one of the most helpful summaries of disability ministry that I have found when she says, "Disability ministry can be understood as a pro-life ministry in the fullest sense of the term. Engaging the lives of individuals and families who are touched by disability shows them that the church is *for* their lives—honoring the image of God in each and every person. Having a vision for special needs ministry that is deeply rooted in the sanctity of human life—in all of its diversity—can be quite energizing. When we realize that those upon whom God has stamped his indelible image are being trodden underfoot by dysfunctional social systems, it should stir our hearts to stamp out discrimination on their behalf. Many people with physical or sensory disabilities are quite effective at advocating for the rights of the disenfranchised in society, and there is much that we can learn from Christians with disabilities who are experienced in this arena. At the same time, many individuals with intellectual disabilities lack the power to be heard. Not only can the Church be the hands and feet of Jesus on behalf of people with intellectual disabilities, but the Church must be the *voice* of Jesus as well. For those individuals who do to have the ability or the power to be heard, others must respectfully step into the gap to speak boldly on their behalf." [52]

It has been an unbelievable joy for our family to have been invited to participate in Joni and Friends ministries, most specifically through their annual Family Retreats offered around the country (and now around the world) each summer. We have participated in seven Family Retreats thus far and are very much looking forward to next year! These retreats are essentially a summer camp experience for families and individuals with disabilities and special needs who might otherwise not have any opportunity to experience that in the traditional way.

Our first Family Retreat was in the summer of 2013 when we were still adjusting to life with Libby and Hannah. I had been invited to serve as the camp pastor that week and our family was invited to participate in the retreat along with dozens of others. It was a dual blessing to be sure as I love being able to pour into others as a minister of the Gospel and to be able to exercise my pastoral gift of teaching. Additionally, it was amazing to be poured into as a family with special needs children, being served, loved, and cared for with the love of Christ by some of the most selfless volunteers on the planet.

The most striking memory I have of that first Family Retreat was the scene in the cafeteria at the first dinner, after all the families had arrived and camp had officially begun. You see, restaurants are a tricky thing for us. First, because our girls each require a wheelchair and we are a family of seven, we take up a lot of space everywhere we go, and we move a lot of furniture and displace a lot of people all in the process of being seated. We are a sight to behold I assure you. Additionally, as I mentioned earlier, our girls squeal, moan, and sometimes flail their arms excitedly and unexpectedly. They drool a lot and are regularly throwing chew toys, bibs, or pacifiers on the floor. We aren't necessarily a casual or quiet crew when we go places. So, for that reason, I'm used to people naturally and most often inquisitively staring at us in public. But not at Family Retreat. Not in the cafeteria at camp. In fact, I was so struck by the anomaly that everyone was just enjoying their dinner and talking and laughing and that a lot of other families were making their own noises and movements, and no one stared. I leaned over with tears in my eyes and told Mary, "We are normal here. This is the first place I feel normal."

Now, the highlight of Family Retreat for me each year is the talent show, held on the last night of camp. Anyone and everyone is invited to participate and share their talent with our entire group. Some are very gifted and others are very passionate, but the entertainment is pure joy and it is without a doubt one of my happiest places on earth. In our first year, a man about forty-five years old with Down syndrome sang, "I Can Only Imagine" for us, to which he received a standing ovation. I was sobbing and cheering, and it was incredible to hear our new friend pour out his heart in this song which tells of a future vision of heaven with God.

And when he finished that song, that is when God spoke to me. Between our family feeling "normal" at dinner and the talent show song of "imagination" that night, God reminded me that this is a snapshot of heaven on earth. Heaven will be a place of perfection, everyone loved and accepted, worshipping Jesus who made it all possible to do so. At places like Family Retreat where for a few days everyone is accepted and loved regardless of their ability or disability, their talent, or their passion, we see a glimpse of the glory of the Gospel that our future in Christ will hold. Randy Alcorn summarizes this glory by saying, "For the Christian, death is not the end of adventure but a doorway to a world where dreams and adventures forever expand. No matter how bad the present, an eternity with Christ in Heaven will be incomparably better. So if *God* thinks the whole thing is worth it—and we know it will be worth it to *us* once we reach Heaven—then why not affirm by faith, even in the midst of suffering, that it's worth it now?" [53]

In the same way that God loves us unconditionally, we get a dimly lit picture of what that love looks like between one another. It's not identical of course, but it paints a glorious picture that I cling to while we are living this life here and now.

Chapter 11

"CHALLENGED"

I grew up playing sports. I love sports. In high school, I played basketball, football, and baseball, but basketball was by far my favorite and what drew the majority of my attention and concentration. Some of my favorite memories in high school revolve around our basketball team. We had a great group of guys. We were all friends and that made practices more tolerable, road trips more fun, and our games more meaningful.

I can still remember our pre-game routines. Once we had gotten taped up and dressed in our uniforms, our coach would give us a brief pep-talk in the locker room, and then we would line up in the back hallway that led into our gym. One highlight that particularly stands out revolves around that celebrated moment of entry into the gym. You see, at our school, every season the senior class of the basketball team was allowed to create the warm-up music. This was a big deal and a great deal of planning and debate went into the selection of every song chosen. This playlist would be played during the pre-game lay-up drills as a way to fire up both the team and the crowd. So we would wait for that familiar music to fire up and then we would excitedly make our way onto the court where our fans would begin cheering and we would hype ourselves up for the challenge ahead. We were pumping ourselves up for the challenge!

Sometimes, I feel like life with our girls requires a pre-game routine over and over again. Mary and I are continually seeking the Lord in prayer and in His Word, getting honest (and vulnerable) with one another, and leaning upon our community of faith, in an attempt to get hyped up for the challenges consistently before us. I can hear the pre-game music from high school in my head even now as I write, and Guns-n-Roses has never sounded so good. But in all honesty, the challenges of suffering are real. They cannot be ignored. They are tough to digest and they are impossible to dismiss.

Some challenges are daily, like managing doctors' appointments and prescription refills and all the detailed administration of medicine, meals, and deeply personal care that our girls require. So much of this is managed and shouldered by Mary, and although she wouldn't tell you about how hard it is or ever complain about the toll it takes, I don't mind saying that it is a full-time job just to keep track of the insurances, therapies, doctors' orders, and government agency requirements which provide our girls the care they so desperately need. It is a challenge.

Other challenges are seasonal, like finding qualified caregivers who can help us take care of Libby and Hannah while we attempt to juggle the schedule, school, games, and activities of three other very busy children and the demands of a fast-growing church. Libby and Hannah are troopers, but it is not feasible for us or best for them to try to force them to make every event on our family calendar.

That's a challenge and at times when it feels burdensome and somewhat overwhelming to navigate, I need the warm-up music of Christ to comfort and hype me up for the need before us.

My greatest challenge (or fear) however is perpetual. While I am confident and certain that our trust remains fully and completely in the Lord as it relates to the long-term prognosis for our daughters, doctors continue to tell us that their life expectancy is very limited. Gratefully, no one attempts to put a timetable on anything anymore, but we are not ignorant of the reality that the girls' diagnosis brings. I cannot sugarcoat this. As their dad, this fear (challenge) has at times consumed me. I am grateful that today it does not control me, but I would also be lying if I said that it has been totally overcome.

In part, I am writing this book in hopes that many of you will see that I do not simply believe because Christ has victoriously overcome sin, death, hell, and the grave, that our lives will therefore be spared any suffering and the subsequent challenges that accompany it. No, suffering is real. The challenge is still before us. And yes, Jesus is still good, God is still sovereign, and Christ has definitively overcome. The reality of our suffering and God's sovereignty are not at odds with one another. On this fallen side of eternity, in our minds, these two things will be a tension we manage and not a problem we solve. God is good, and yes, His children still suffer. It's challenging, but it's true. In fact, this truth is the very center of the Christian faith, as author Tim Keller reminds us, "Suffering is at the very heart of the Christian faith. It is not only the way Christ became like and redeemed us, but it is one of the main ways we become like him and experience his redemption. And that means that our suffering, despite its painfulness, is also filled with purpose and usefulness." [54]

I have discovered in our story, and having been "counted worthy," our challenge serves as our confession. I don't know what is ahead for our family. I don't know how long God will allow my daughters (or anyone else) to live on earth. I don't know what the next trauma is going to be. I don't know if the seizures will ever stop. I don't know if we will be back in the hospital this year. I don't know what risks new viruses pose and what are the right precautions to take. I don't know if the girls' insurance benefits will ever be maxed out and leave us in a financial crisis. I don't know if there will be a day where Mary and I can no longer safely care for them at home. I don't know the answers to these challenges.

I confess, however, what I do know. I know God is good. I know that Jesus is enough. I know that the Bible is true and has proven its reliability in my life over and over again. I know that Mary is exactly who I am supposed to be married to today and exactly who has been entrusted as the mother to my kids because she is. I know God is in control of all things. I know the Church of the Lord Jesus Christ is the greatest gift for ministering hope to the broken people and circumstances of this world that there is. I know that God is working amid all suffering, ours included. I know that on THIS day, there will be a THAT day, and on THAT day, God will redeem and renew and restore all that sin and Satan have stolen and destroyed.

I'm trying my best to maintain my joy and trust in Jesus for this day. I appreciate the Scriptural challenge Randy Alcorn gives, when he writes, "Scripture commands us to rejoice in suffering because of the perseverance it produces in us. Like James (in 1:2–3), Paul said, 'We also rejoice in our sufferings, because we know that suffering produces perseverance' (Romans 5:3). Paul and James both claim that we should rejoice in suffering because of what it produces: *perseverance*.

"Adversity itself doesn't cause our joy. Rather, our joy comes in the expectation of adversity's by-product, the development of godly character. God doesn't ask us to cheer because we lose our job, or a loved one contracts cancer, or a child has an incurable birth defect. He tells us to rejoice because he will produce in us something money can't buy and ease will never produce—the precious quality of Christ-exalting perseverance." [55]

I've heard it said before that we should not trade what we don't know for what we do know. I know there are great challenges in our life and in our family. I know there will be more. I know that suffering for us and the sovereignty of God are both very real and true.

I know that you, too, will have challenges. And I want to challenge you as you meet them. If you can embrace joy and develop a "counted worthy" mindset, then your challenges will become your confession as well. God is writing a story in the midst of your suffering. Perhaps you need this chapter of this book to hype you up like a pre-game lay-up line as you prepare for whatever it is you are facing next. There are a lot of things you don't know, that is for sure. There are also a lot of things you do know, that is also for sure. Guard your heart against trading what you don't for what you do.

So, if you will indulge me ... I would like to be the DJ for your lay-up line. And the playlist I've put together for you comes directly from the Word of God. Yes, you are facing a challenge, but a hope in God is how you're going to face whatever that happens to be. *"May the God of hope fill you with all joy and peace in believing, so that by the power of the Holy Spirit you may abound in hope"* (Romans 15:13 ESV). The apostle Paul talks about a couple of things. The first is the power of the Holy Spirit at work in the lives of us as God's children. The second is that the evidence of this power and the passionate plea for this desire is that it (HOPE) would abound in our lives as God's children. And this word *abound* that is used in conjunction with hope, it carries with it the idea of *hope overflowing*. That by the power of God's Spirit, Paul is asking God to provide an absolutely embarrassing plethora of hope. Unshakable hope. And so when thinking about how this works practically in our lives, we must understand that our hope is sourced in God. And as it relates to our suffering, God *redeems* it.

In the book, *Why, O God?*, the author beautifully summarizes this truth when she writes, "God redeems suffering. The God of life is the only one who can conquer death by embracing it. And so death no longer has the victory, and neither does suffering. Christ has given it meaning, not only for salvation but also for sanctification, and that is the best part. It tells us we are no longer alone in our hardships, our disabilities. Our suffering is not a flip of the coin; it is not a fluke of fate. We are not in the middle of some divine cosmic accident. No, our suffering can be *redeemed*. Oh, the wonder of such a thought is that it is all for our sanctification, our relationship with Him, and our witness to a world in need of redemption." [56]

This is how we prepare for every game, every day, every season, every storm, and face each challenge, however difficult they may be. Our hope finds its substance in Jesus. And our hope is supplied by the Holy Spirit, which is how we can be confident while we long for something greater in our future. So, here's hoping that you always remember:

- *"He who began a good work in you will bring it to completion at the day of Christ Jesus"* (Philippians 1:6).

- *"He will never leave you or forsake you"* (Deuteronomy 31:6).

- *"If we confess our sins, He is faithful and just to forgive us and to cleanse us of all unrighteousness"* (1 John 1:9).

- *"If we confess with our mouths that Jesus is Lord and believe in our hearts that God raised him from the grave, we will be saved"* (Romans 10:10).

- *"For I am sure that neither death nor life, nor angels nor rulers, nor things present nor things to come, nor powers, nor height nor depth, nor anything else in all creation, will be able to separate us from the love of God in Christ Jesus our Lord"* (Romans 8:38–39)"

So… *"Why are you cast down, O my soul, and why are you in turmoil within me? Hope in God; for I shall again praise him, my salvation and my God"* (Psalm 42:5–6a ESV).

Friend, you have been counted worthy by the God of the universe to steward this season of suffering for as long as God has determined it will be. That challenge is also your confession. It is your opportunity to tell of what you believe, to whom you belong, and where your trust is found. It is not easy, but it is possible with God. Anything is possible with God. You can do this. You are not alone. God is with you. The Church of the Lord Jesus Christ can be a gift to you. God has men and women who will walk beside you. If you reach out and share your struggle with me, I will commit to pray for you. God sees you. God hears you. He has not forgotten you. If you're in Christ you're going to win. You've got this. God loves you. Always, forever, He loves you.

References

1. Tripp, Paul David, *Suffering: Gospel Hope When Life Doesn't Make Sense* (Wheaton, IL: Crossway, 2018) 23-24.

2. Chandler, Matt, *Joy in the Sorrow: How a Thriving Church (and its Pastor) Learned to Suffer Well* (London, UK: The Good Book Company, 2019) 19-20.

3. Ibid, 20.

4. Tripp, Paul David, *Suffering: Gospel Hope When Life Doesn't Make Sense* (Wheaton, IL: Crossway, 2018) 157.

5. Hubach, Stephanie O., *Same Lake Different Boat: Coming Alongside People Touched by Disability* (Phillipsburg, NJ: P&R Publishing Company, 2006) 47.

6. Alcorn, Randy, *If God is Good: Faith in the Midst of Suffering and Evil* (Colorado Springs, CO: Multnomah Books, 2009) 213.

7. Hubach, Stephanie O., *Same Lake Different Boat: Coming Alongside People Touched by Disability* (Phillipsburg, NJ: P&R Publishing Company, 2006) 85.

8. Tripp, Paul David, *Suffering: Gospel Hope When Life Doesn't Make Sense* (Wheaton, IL: Crossway, 2018) 31.

9. Ibid, 125.

10. Larry J. Waters and Roy B. Zuck, *Why, O God?: Suffering and Disability in the Bible and the Church* (Wheaton, IL: Crossway, 2011) 83.

11. Alcorn, Randy, *If God is Good: Faith in the Midst of Suffering and Evil* (Colorado Springs, CO: Multnomah Books, 2009) 453.

12. Powlison, David, *God's Grace in Your Suffering* (Wheaton, IL: Crossway, 2018) 45-46.

13. Vroegop, Mark, *Dark Clouds, Deep Mercy: Discovering the Grace of Lament* (Wheaton, IL: Crossway, 2019) 47.

14. Keller, Timothy, *Walking with God through Pain and Suffering* (New York, NY: Penguin Random House LLC, 2013) 193.

15. John Piper and Justin Taylor, *Suffering and the Sovereignty of God* (Wheaton, IL: Crossway, 2006) 166.

16. Alcorn, Randy, *If God is Good: Faith in the Midst of Suffering and Evil* (Colorado Springs, CO: Multnomah Books, 2009) 429.

17. Larry J. Waters and Roy B. Zuck, *Why, O God?: Suffering and Disability in the Bible and the Church* (Wheaton, IL: Crossway, 2011) 111.

18. Hubach, Stephanie O., *Same Lake Different Boat: Coming Alongside People Touched by Disability* (Phillipsburg, NJ: P&R Publishing Company, 2006) 49.

19. Elliot, Elisabeth, *Suffering is Never for Nothing* (Nashville, TN: B&H Publishing Group, 2019) 59.

20. D.A. Carson and Kathleen Nielson, *Resurrection Life in a World of Suffering* (Wheaton, IL: Crossway, 2018) 53.

21. Furman, Dave, *Kiss the Wave: Embracing God in Your Trials* (Wheaton, IL: Crossway, 2018) 96.

22. Keller, Timothy, *Walking with God through Pain and Suffering* (New York, NY: Penguin Random House LLC, 2013) 135.

23. Alcorn, Randy, *If God is Good: Faith in the Midst of Suffering and Evil* (Colorado Springs, CO: Multnomah Books, 2009) 394-395.

24. Hubach, Stephanie O., *Same Lake Different Boat: Coming Alongside People Touched by Disability* (Phillipsburg, NJ: P&R Publishing Company, 2006) 31-32.

25. Tripp, Paul David, *Suffering: Gospel Hope When Life Doesn't Make Sense* (Wheaton, IL: Crossway, 2018) 109.

26. Furman, Dave, *Kiss the Wave: Embracing God in Your Trials* (Wheaton, IL: Crossway, 2018) 45-46.

27. Joni Eareckson Tada and Steven Estes, *When God Weeps: Why Our Sufferings Matter to the Almighty* (Grand Rapids, MI: Zondervan, 1997) 115.

28. Tada, Joni Eareckson, *A Place of Healing: Wrestling with the Mysteries of Suffering, Pain, and God's Sovereignty* (Colorado Springs, CO: David C. Cook, 2010) 57.

29. John Piper and Justin Taylor, *Suffering and the Sovereignty of God* (Wheaton, IL: Crossway, 2006) 189-190.

30. Vroegop, Mark, *Dark Clouds, Deep Mercy: Discovering the Grace of Lament* (Wheaton, IL: Crossway, 2019) 193.

31. Keller, Timothy, *Walking with God through Pain and Suffering* (New York, NY: Penguin Random House LLC, 2013) 117.

32. Furman, Dave, *Kiss the Wave: Embracing God in Your Trials* (Wheaton, IL: Crossway, 2018) 65.

33. Elliot, Elisabeth, *Suffering is Never for Nothing* (Nashville, TN: B&H Publishing Group, 2019) 1-2.

34. Tripp, Paul David, *Suffering: Gospel Hope When Life Doesn't Make Sense* (Wheaton, IL: Crossway, 2018) 34.

35. Powlison, David, *God's Grace in Your Suffering* (Wheaton, IL: Crossway, 2018) 21.

36. Elliot, Elisabeth, *Through Gates of Splendor* (Carol Stream, IL: Tyndale, 1996) 263.

37. Elliot, Elisabeth, *Suffering is Never for Nothing* (Nashville, TN: B&H Publishing Group, 2019) 9.

38. Chandler, Matt, *Joy in the Sorrow: How a Thriving Church (and its Pastor) Learned to Suffer Well* (London, UK: The Good Book Company, 2019) 169-170.

39. Powlison, David, *God's Grace in Your Suffering* (Wheaton, IL: Crossway, 2018) 52.

40. Larry J. Waters and Roy B. Zuck, *Why, O God?: Suffering and Disability in the Bible and the Church* (Wheaton, IL: Crossway, 2011) 233.

41. Alcorn, Randy, *If God is Good: Faith in the Midst of Suffering and Evil* (Colorado Springs, CO: Multnomah Books, 2009) 365-366.

42. Ibid, 27.

43. Keller, Timothy, *Walking with God through Pain and Suffering* (New York, NY: Penguin Random House LLC, 2013) 29-30.

44. Joni Eareckson Tada and Steven Estes, *When God Weeps: Why Our Sufferings Matter to the Almighty* (Grand Rapids, MI: Zondervan, 1997) 125.

45. Keller, Timothy, *Walking with God through Pain and Suffering* (New York, NY: Penguin Random House LLC, 2013) 158.

46. Furman, Dave, *Kiss the Wave: Embracing God in Your Trials* (Wheaton, IL: Crossway, 2018) 42.

47. Tada, Joni Eareckson, *A Place of Healing: Wrestling with the Mysteries of Suffering, Pain, and God's Sovereignty* (Colorado Springs, CO: David C. Cook, 2010) 239-240.

48. Alcorn, Randy, *If God is Good: Faith in the Midst of Suffering and Evil* (Colorado Springs, CO: Multnomah Books, 2009) 209.

49. Vroegop, Mark, *Dark Clouds, Deep Mercy: Discovering the Grace of Lament* (Wheaton, IL: Crossway, 2019) 32-33.

50. Tripp, Paul David, *Suffering: Gospel Hope When Life Doesn't Make Sense* (Wheaton, IL: Crossway, 2018) 201.

51. Alcorn, Randy, *If God is Good: Faith in the Midst of Suffering and Evil* (Colorado Springs, CO: Multnomah Books, 2009) 488.

52. Hubach, Stephanie O., *Same Lake Different Boat: Coming Alongside People Touched by Disability* (Phillipsburg, NJ: P&R Publishing Company, 2006) 200.

53. Alcorn, Randy, *If God is Good: Faith in the Midst of Suffering and Evil* (Colorado Springs, CO: Multnomah Books, 2009) 202.

54. Keller, Timothy, *Walking with God through Pain and Suffering* (New York, NY: Penguin Random House LLC, 2013) 163-164.

55. Alcorn, Randy, *If God is Good: Faith in the Midst of Suffering and Evil* (Colorado Springs, CO: Multnomah Books, 2009) 426.

56. Larry J. Waters and Roy B. Zuck, *Why, O God?: Suffering and Disability in the Bible and the Church* (Wheaton, IL: Crossway, 2011) 17-18.

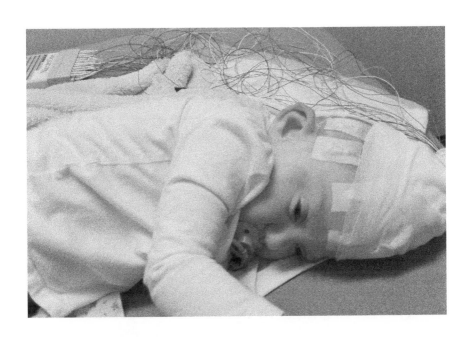

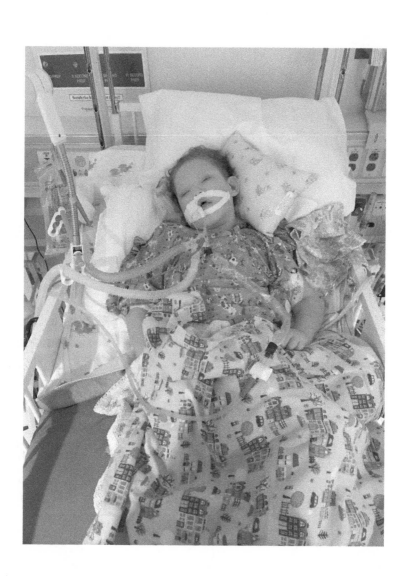

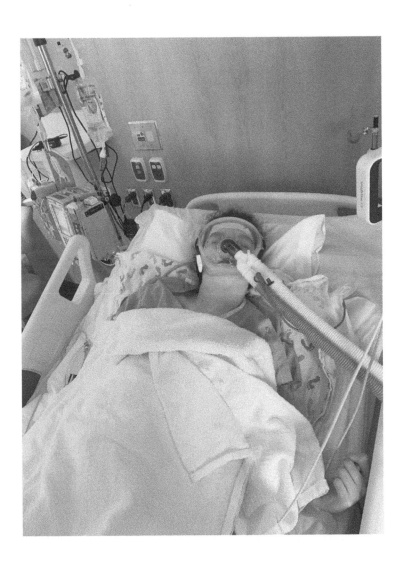

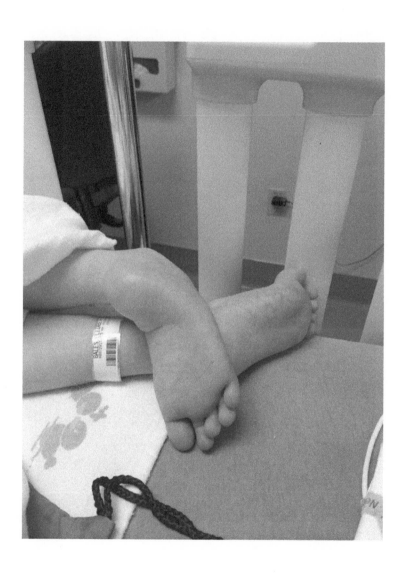